Susan
September 9--7

EXPLOR
WARWICKS
WILD PLA---

CW00516564

*A Guide to the Best Wildlife Sites and Places of
Natural Beauty in the County.*

LINDA BARNETT AND CRAIG EMMS

S.B. Publications

I came across this book & found the
walks & wild life association fascinating.
Enjoy.   Valerie Ian

This book is dedicated to Alice, Bill, Richard and Andrew Emms, and Mavis, Yvonne, Samantha and Sophie Barnett.

First published in 1998 by S.B.Publications
c/o 19 Grove Road, Seaford, East Sussex, BN25 1TP

© Copyright 1998 Linda Barnett and Craig Emms

All rights reserved. No part of this publication may be reproduced, stored in a retrieval system or transmitted in any form or by any means, electronic, mechanical, photocopying, recording or otherwise, without the prior permission of the publishers.

ISBN 1 85770 160 7

Typeset and printed by Island Press,
3 Cradle Hill Industrial Estate, Seaford, East Sussex BN25 3JE
Telephone: 01323 490222 UK

Front Cover: Crackley Wood Local Nature Reserve
Title Page: Brandon Marsh Nature Reserve

All photographs by Dr Linda K Barnett

Contents

Foreword

Having had the immense pleasure of the company of the authors while surveying remote islands in the Indian Ocean I know you are in for a treat. They are natural historians in the true sense of the words, full of knowledge and wonder about all living things. Their special forte being the insects - indeed Linda is known to all her many friends as the 'Butterfly Lady'.

Now if anyone is questioning the existence of wild places in Warwickshire, be ready to be surprised and pleased. All is about to be revealed, habitat by habitat, for this super little book is about to take you on a safari of exploration in deepest greenest Warwickshire. From rivers, streams and wetlands to the dizzy heights of grassland and ancient woodland. Enroute you will be joined by birds and butterflies, mammals small and not so small, the march of the seasons, the scent of wild flowers and the buzz of biodiversity.

When enough of their infectious enthusiasm has rubbed off, the field is yours with maps and notes, enough to get there so you can see it, hear it, smell it, and even touch it all for yourself.

Never again will you have the excuse of not knowing the names and the strange habits of your natural neighbours and the way of getting to know them better. There is even a section on parks and gardens which can be havens for our local wildlife, if only we care enough. The Warwickshire Wildlife Trust certainly care enough and if you aren't a member I suggest you join. Happy reading, happy spotting and as you do, take only photographs and be careful where you leave your footprints.

David Bellamy
Bedburn 1997.

Preface

Warwickshire is situated in the heart of England. It has been influenced by many factors, especially its peoples, who in the last 100 years have changed the face of the county and more or less everything growing within it. The most significant changes have been brought about by the urbanisation of the Black Country with Birmingham and Coventry which together have a population of some three million inhabitants. These changes have resulted in the need to build new homes, new factories, new roads and new areas for leisure activities.

Side by side with this urbanisation have been the changes brought about in agriculture to produce more food with the use of pesticides and fertilisers. Woods, meadows, hedgerows and ponds have disappeared with the consequent loss of all important habitats for wild life. Yet in spite of all these changes fragments of the former countryside remain and these are of tremendous value for wild life. Many of these are also areas of outstanding natural beauty. They contain a surprising number of species, both plant and animal. To actually discover and look closely at a 'new' species for the first time is so much more exciting than viewing a photograph which someone else has taken. To wander along a woodland path in spring with the slanting rays of the sun between the trees high-lighting up patches of wild Primroses is a sight to be cherished.

The authors are to be congratulated in producing this guide which is of immense practical value for the beginner as well as the experienced field naturalist.

Mont Hirons
Banbury 1997

Introduction

Warwickshire, like many other counties in Britain, is no longer covered with its original vegetation. The countryside that we see today is the result of thousands of years of occupancy by people. Humankind has altered the landscape to suit its own needs. It is now a mosaic of vegetation ranging from the entirely artificial (such as agricultural fields and plantation woodlands) to modified semi-natural habitats (such as flowering meadows and ancient woodlands). There are no truly 'wild places' left in Warwickshire. But for the dedicated naturalist, or the person who just wants to take a pleasant and peaceful stroll through the countryside, there are some places that are 'wilder' than others. It is in these places that plentiful wildlife can still be found.

We have written this book to help you explore the top fifteen wildlife sites in the county, and learn about the different habitats associated with them. For ten of the sites we have given details of how to get there, but have left you to explore on your own. We have also given guidance on the specialities that may be seen during different times of the year. For five other sites, we have provided detailed guided walks, pointing out aspects of the natural history along the way. By providing this variety we hope to include people who enjoy a simple walk in the countryside, the novice in the field and the Warwickshire wildlife expert who may find some new discoveries in their county. In the gazetteer, we have listed an additional fifty sites in Warwickshire, with their main groups of interest, for those who like to explore the countryside in more depth. Details of the different sites referenced in the text can be found in the gazetteer.

To achieve clarity when referring to species we have capitalised the names of individual species but not those of collections of species. For example the Tawny Owl is one of several owls found in Warwickshire, the other owls being the Barn Owl, Short-eared Owl, Long-eared Owl and Little Owl.

We hope that you enjoy reading this book as much as we have enjoyed writing it. Happy exploring!

Habitats of Warwickshire

Warwickshire has a wide range of habitats. These include various forms of wetland (e.g. rivers, streams, ponds, lakes, canals and marshes), grasslands (e.g. 'improved' grassland, pasture, damp meadows, and tall herb), woodlands (e.g. scrub, willow/alder carr, ancient woodland and plantation woodland) and urban habitat (e.g. post industrial, parks, recreational areas and gardens). Many of these habitats contain an astonishing diversity of plants and animals. However these species are not randomly distributed but are often found in 'groups' of associated flora and fauna. The same (or similar) species occur wherever the same physical conditions exist and form distinctive living communities within each habitat type. This chapter describes the major types of habitat that can be found in Warwickshire, and some of the plants and animals that are associated with them.

Wetlands

Rivers and Streams

Rivers and streams are important freshwater habitats for many species of flora and fauna. The variety of animals and plants found in them is affected by the nature of the landscape that the water passes through, the physical structure of the river or stream (including the shape of its banks and the nature of the material present on the bottom) and the rate at which water flows in it.

Slow flowing rivers with shallow and heavily vegetated banks are often good places to see a range of damselflies and dragonflies

In the past many of our rivers have suffered quite badly when we have tried to change their direction and the rate of water flow in them. We have straightened, deepened and widened them, mostly to control their natural flooding patterns and their influence over the land around them. Such action has done much to change the characters of our rivers and has drastically lessened their value for wildlife. However, attitudes are changing and national projects now exist which aim to restore parts of our rivers back to a more natural state. The best rivers are those that have a diverse structure, with some fast-flowing shallow riffles but also deep pools and eddies. Good examples of these include the River Avon - especially in the Stoneleigh area, the River Arrow in the west of the county, and the River Sowe which flows through the city of Coventry.

The structure of the river bank is also important and those rivers with the most diverse types of bank are often the best for wildlife. Steep vertical banks are ideal places for Kingfishers to excavate their nest tunnels. At the other extreme, shallow banks with a low gradient are excellent for a wide range of marginal plants such as sedges, rushes, reeds, Purple Loosestrife and Yellow Flag. These plants in turn allow the aquatic nymph stages of insects like the Banded Demoiselle and Brown Hawker dragonfly to haul themselves from the water and change into adult flying insects.

Yellow Flag

Our rivers are inhabited by large numbers of fish, including Gudgeon, Chub, Dace, Roach, Rudd and Barbel. These provide food for birds like the Grey Heron, Little Grebe and Cormorant. Fish are also the main food of the Otter, which is thankfully making a slow but steady comeback into our rivers from the west. This charming animal has been recently seen at Brandon Marsh Nature Reserve, just to the south-east of Coventry.

Ponds and Lakes

Ponds are widely distributed throughout Warwickshire but appear to have suffered a general decline in both quantity and quality over the last century. They were once common, especially in agricultural land, and played an important role in the watering of domestic life-stock. These days they are less important as watering holes but they do play an enormous role in safe-guarding our populations of aquatic plants and animals, especially all of our amphibians. A great variety of aquatic and terrestrial plants occur in and around ponds, including the common Canadian

8

Waterweed, Water Plantain and Amphibious Bistort. As well as frogs, toads and newts, the harmless Grass Snake is often associated with ponds, and is a very good swimmer. It is recognised by its yellow or cream coloured collar over an olive-green body. It is not as common as it once was, but it is still possible to encounter some very large specimens of Grass Snake, up to two metres or so in length. In addition ponds are refuges for many insects, including dragonflies and damselflies, both of which require water to complete their life cycles. Southern Hawker and Emperor dragonflies and Common Blue Damselflies are commonly seen flying above and resting on vegetation beside and emerging from ponds.

Coombe Lake was created in the 1770s by Lancelot 'Capability' Brown by the simple method of damming the Smite Brook

Ponds need careful and consistent management to remain good habitats for wildlife, as they can soon become clogged with aquatic vegetation, turn into marsh and then gradually dry out. One positive aspect of many new building developments (such as around the grounds of the University of Warwick) is that new ponds are often created as ornamental water features. With forethought and care many of these can be turned into wildlife havens, helping to offset the loss of more natural sites.

There are no large naturally occurring lakes in Warwickshire. However there are a small number of old man-made lakes in deer parks and private estates. An excellent example can be found at Coombe Abbey Country Park. Lakes such as these are very rich in wildlife. They have shallow banks which are home to many emergent and marginal wetland plants. These shallows also act as nurseries and feeding places for many species of fish. It is therefore no accident that Coombe is the home to the largest heronry in Warwickshire.

Man-made lakes also come in the form of reservoirs, and increasingly these days, as flooded sand or gravel pits. Fine examples of these can be seen at Shustoke Reservoir, Brandon Marsh Nature Reserve and Ryton Pools Country Park. Draycote Reservoir is the largest reservoir in the county and like all large areas of water, is attractive to birds. Many of these places are thus important sites for water birds such as swans, geese, ducks, grebes and gulls, both as wintering sites and as areas for breeding to take place in the summer.

The large pool at Ryton Pools Country Park is a popular place for both the birds and public

Canals

Canals are artificial waterways that were constructed for various functions including navigation, irrigation and water power. They resemble lakes and ponds rather than rivers in the types of plants and animals that are found in them, because of their slower water flow. Warwickshire is traversed by a number of canals which have been with us for over a century. These include the Coventry Canal, the Oxford Canal, the Stratford-on-Avon Canal and the Grand Union Canal. Many of these penetrate the hearts of Warwickshire's major cities as well as traversing the countryside.

Fish that are often found in canals include Pike, Gudgeon, Roach and Tench. Great Crested Newts, Smooth Newts, the Common Frog and Common Toad also

The Oxford Canal beside Newbold Quarry Park

11

occur in this habitat, the latter three being much more common. Coventry Canal, in particular, has good populations of the Smooth Newt.

Many more species live in the range of habitats that can be found near the tow path beside canals. Moorhens and Kingfishers are often seen here. During the harsher climate of the winter, Grey Herons are also regularly seen fishing near the unfrozen areas under canal bridges. A less easily observed inhabitant is the Water Vole. This is a small rodent that is often confused with the Brown Rat (though the water vole has none of the bad habits that are associated with the rat). It is often seen swimming strongly along the canal to take refuge in one of its many waterside tunnels on the bank.

Marshes

When ponds and pools become choked with vegetation they eventually dry out and change into marsh. This happens because the dead leaves and stalks of plants gradually build up in ponds until the standing water becomes very shallow. It is then that plants like Common Reed or Reedmace will take over, and often marshlands are entirely composed of one or two species like these. Marshes have become rarer these days as they are often drained to make way for development or agricultural reclamation. They have a very distinct flora and fauna, and several species, such as some of the Wainscot moths, are found in no other habitat. Many other animals and birds, including the Reed Warbler, Sedge Warbler and Water Rail, breed in reed-beds. Cuckoos are attracted to reed-beds to lay their eggs in the nests of warblers. Birds of prey, such as Marsh and Hen Harriers, and the Short-eared Owl, can often be seen quartering large expenses of marshland, especially in the winter, for small mammals and birds. Good areas of marsh occur at Whitacre Heath Nature Reserve and Kingsbury Water Park, located in the Tame Valley in the north of Warwickshire.

Often mistakenly called 'Bullrushes' these plants are in fact Reedmace, and are typical of marshy areas

Grasslands

Meadows and Calcareous Grassland

At one time the countryside of Warwickshire was filled with flowering meadows. These were ablaze with the colour of numerous wild flower species and hummed with insect and bird life. Such diverse areas of grassland were created through the traditional management practice of hay making, which provided food for livestock in the winter. Hay meadows were not fertilised in any way. Indeed it was the poor quality of the soil that resulted in the diversity of flowers and grasses.

Today only a few old meadows of outstanding quality remain in Warwickshire. These have survived being 'improved' for animal grazing or silage production and the consequent treatment by fertilisers and herbicides. Draycote Meadows is probably the finest of these and contains thousands of Green-winged Orchids in early summer. These orchids put on a magnificent display for visitors, alongside other rare plants like Yellow Rattle, Cowslip and Adder's Tongue Fern. Draycote is also the last remaining site in the county for a fern with the splendid name of Moonwort. Other, smaller, meadows still survive in odd corners, like the tiny Harvest Hill Nature Reserve to the north-west of Coventry (where Wild Daffodils can still be seen in large numbers in spring), Deans Green and Stonebridge Meadows Local Nature Reserve. The latter site has Harebell and many other uncommon plants growing in acid grassland.

Wild Daffodils are smaller and more delicate than cultivated varieties. They can be seen in large numbers at Harvest Hill Nature Reserve to the north-west of Coventry

Spectacular areas of wild flowers can also be seen on calcareous grassland. They grow on lime-rich soils over chalk or in old limestone quarries such as can be found at Ufton Fields Nature Reserve and Country Park. Here Yellow Wort, Ox-eye Daisy, Kidney Vetch and Wild Basil grow alongside six species of Orchid. Butterflies abound at Ufton, especially the Marbled White in July and Small Blue, Dingy and Grizzled Skippers in May and June. These beautiful insects were once a very common sight in our countryside but have declined in numbers with the meadows where they once thrived. The most typical butterfly of old meadows is the Meadow Brown. This common and handsome insect feeds as a caterpillar on grasses. Other inhabitants of meadows during the summer include brightly-coloured day-flying moths like the burnets and the Cinnabar, and birds like the wonderfully melodious Skylark.

Purple Loosestrife is a beautiful native plant that often grows by the edges of rivers or in damp meadows

Damp Meadows

Damp meadows or 'water meadows' are often flooded in the winter and they may be several metres under water at times, forming small lakes. The flora of these meadows is heavily influenced by such periods of inundation, and comprise species that are well adapted to these conditions such as rushes, sedges, Purple Loosestrife and Meadowsweet - a tall plant with creamy fragrant flower heads. Damp meadows are also a haven for various types of bird, especially in the winter. Large flocks of Lapwings and Golden Plover will often frequent this habitat before it becomes flooded. When covered with water, birds such as geese and ducks can be found, along with large flocks of Black-headed, Common, Herring and Lesser Black-backed Gulls. Wading birds such as Green and Common Sandpipers, Snipe and Redshank can sometimes be seen probing the soil for their invertebrate food along the shallower edges.

Damp meadows were once a common feature along the river valleys of Warwickshire. Although this habitat is less common today, an example can still be found at Welches Meadow Local Nature Reserve in Leamington.

'Improved' Grassland and Pasture

Many old meadows, whether damp, dry, neutral or calcareous, have been changed beyond recognition by modern farming techniques. With the sole aim to increase their productivity for cattle and sheep grazing or silage, old meadows have been ploughed up and re-seeded with fast-growing grasses and treated with fertilisers and herbicides, producing vast areas of 'improved' grassland and pasture. In addition hedgerows have often been removed to increase the size of fields, so that modern machinery can move more easily in them, and the farmer can gain a few more square metres of productive farmland.

Most of our countryside is now made up of such grassland. On the surface it may appear to be rich and green. However such fields of improved meadow and pasture are in fact very poor for wildlife and have frequently been referred to as 'green deserts' by nature conservationists. The wildlife commonly seen in this type of habitat includes hedgerow birds such as the Yellowhammer, Chaffinch, Blackbird and Woodpigeon, and animals that take refuge in the remaining ancient hedgerows, for example Foxes, Rabbits and Field Voles (especially along the field margin if the grass is left uncut). Ancient hedgerows are often the last refuges of wild flowers, birds and other animals in such an increasingly sterile countryside. They are brimming with food for wildlife, for example flowers bursting with nectar and heavy crops of nuts, berries and seeds. Sadly, the hedges that are left often suffer from herbicidal and insecticide sprays that drift onto them when the fields are treated on windy days.

On the surface improved grasslands look green and inviting, but they are generally empty of wildlife compared to more traditionally managed areas such as meadows

Recent legislation may protect ancient hedgerows from further losses, and a hint of good news is that many hedges are being replanted, though these will take a very long time to mature enough to be good wildlife habitat.

Common Ragwort is a typical plant of the tall herb community and buzzes with insects. Here a Meadow Brown butterfly nectars on ragwort flowers while a Cinnabar moth caterpillar eats its leaves

Tall Herb

Tall herb can be found almost anywhere and is a much under-rated habitat for wildlife. Tall herb describes the type of vegetation that grows on waste land, at the bottom of hedgerows or along roads, railways or river-sides. The plants that can be found in these habitats vary greatly according to the soil type, but commonly found species include Common Nettle, docks, thistles and ragworts. These sites often look untidy during the latter part of the year, when the plants - which are mostly annuals - begin to die down. In contrast, in the spring and summer they can be packed with flowers and buzzing with insect life. Tall herbs usually produce vast quantities of seeds and these in turn act as a magnet to draw in large numbers of seed-eating birds like Tree Sparrows, finches and buntings. They also sustain high populations of small mammals like the Field Vole and Harvest Mouse. These small birds and mammals in turn attract the attentions of predatory birds such as the Kestrel. This bird is a familiar sight in the Warwickshire countryside, often along roadsides, seeming to hang motionless in the air as it scans the ground below for its prey.

Woodlands

Scrub and Willow/Alder Carr

In the process of natural vegetation succession, the fine grasses and flowering plants of grassland and tall herb communities are replaced with taller more woody species of plants like Elder, Blackthorn and hawthorn. In time these woody plants will grow taller and thicker and will shade out the other plants completely until they form a thicket-like habitat, known as scrub. Scrub is the precursor to mature woodland and the plants that make up scrub are vigorous. Even wetland areas can be gradually shaded out by this habitat, (although this is often by species of shrubs and trees that are more tolerant of damp soil, like Alder or the various types of willow). When scrub is formed on damp soil it is known as 'carr'. Scrub and carr are great habitats for many creatures, supplying them with nutritious food supplies in the form of seeds and fruits such as crab apples, rose-hips and haws, and the berries of Bramble, Elder, Rowan, Holly and Guelder Rose. During the winter huge flocks of Fieldfares, Redwings, Siskins and Redpolls migrate from the colder temperatures in the north of Europe and descend on patches of scrub in search of this abundant food supply. In some years they are joined by small numbers of the very handsome Waxwing.

Alder 'cones' which look very much like miniature pine cones, are eagerly sought by birds, at first for their seeds, then later because they shelter large numbers

As one of the earliest shrubs to come into flower, Blackthorn is a magnet to numerous kinds of insects that nectar on its fragrant blossoms

of insects. In spring, hawthorn and Blackthorn trees become heavy with fragrant blossom and these are the favourite nectar sources for early-flying insects. During the summer the impenetrable, and often thorny thickets are a popular place for birds to build their nests.

Scrub is a fairly common habitat in many parts of Warwickshire and can be found on the edges of woods and in other areas where active management of the land has stopped. The 'old meadows' in Ryton Wood Nature Reserve are formed by scrub that has re-colonised a patch of the woodland that was once cleared for agriculture. It is believed that this area was abandoned as farmland during the time of the 'Black Death' in the 14th century. Good sites to see Willow carr include Brandon Marsh and Whitacre Heath Nature Reserves. An excellent area of mature Alder carr can be found at Stonebridge Meadows Nature Reserve to the south of Coventry.

Ancient Woodland

Nowadays, the old adage of 'leafy' Warwickshire is perhaps a misnomer. Less than three percent of the county is wooded, although half of this is ancient woodland. The term 'ancient semi-natural woodland' describes land that has borne trees since at least 1600 AD. Such woods have a great variety of wildlife compared to modern woodlands and plantations of exotic conifers. The ancient woodlands of Warwickshire are characterised by their plant species (which are themselves determined by the soil type), and the age structure of the species present in the wood. The latter feature is the result of previous and current woodland management (e.g. coppicing and woodland ride creation).

In the north-western half of the county, the soil is more acidic and less fertile, whereas in the south it is richer and more alkaline. This contrast causes a

Yellow Archangel - an indicator species of ancient woodland

difference in woodland types. Woods in the north west are made up of Sessile and Pedunculate Oak, Small-leaved Lime and both Silver and Downy Birches. Rowan, Holly and Buckthorn make up the under storey. Examples of such woods include Ryton Wood, Piles Coppice, Clowes Wood and Crackley Wood. In the south Ash is often the dominant species. Pedunculate Oak is less frequent, and Sessile Oak is absent. The shrub layer is made up of Dogwood, Hazel, Wayfaring Tree and Midland Hawthorn. Examples of such woods include Snitterfield Bushes and Hampton Wood.

The rich ground flora of ancient woodland is at its best in the spring. Carpets of Bluebells combine with patches of Wood Anemone, Wood Sorrel, Red Campion and Common Dog Violet to make a colourful display. Yellow Archangel, Lesser Celandine and Primrose add a dramatic contrast of form and colour. Lily-of-the valley flourishes at Clowes wood, along with Common Cow-wheat and Bilberry. The woods of the south typically support a more diverse flora than those of the north-west, with the lime in the soil encouraging many orchids like the Early Purple Orchid which complements the Bluebells in many places.

As well as being home to a great variety of flora, ancient woodlands probably support a richer variety of animal life than any other British habitat. Species commonly encountered during the day include Sparrowhawk, Tawny Owl, Great Spotted and Green Woodpeckers, Treecreeper, Nuthatch, Blue, Great and Long Tailed Tits, Wren, Robin, Dunnock, Chaffinch, Bullfinch and Blackbird, Mole, Common and Pigmy Shrews, Rabbit, Red Fox, Grey Squirrel, Bank Vole, Wood Mouse and Chinese Muntjac Deer. Butterflies include the common Speckled Wood and the less common White Admiral.

The Common Shrew - this animal is a voracious eater consuming huge quantities of worms, beetles, caterpillars and woodlice

19

Ancient woodlands such as Ryton Wood Nature Reserve are one of the richest habitats for wildlife in the Warwickshire countryside and are a pleasure to walk through at any time of the year

In contrast to many ancient woodlands, conifer plantations such as this one are dark and gloomy and contain a small range of wildlife

Plantation Woodland

Plantation woodland can consist of broad-leafed woodland, coniferous woodland or a mixture of both. Many of the large birds and animals commonly seen in this type of habitat are the same as those seen in ancient woodland, since many are mobile and they will seek refuge in less diverse woodland. Plantations of exotic conifers are however generally poor in other forms of wildlife. Mature pines support a restricted range of birds including the Goldcrest and Coal Tit.

Many woodlands in Warwickshire have been recently planted. Unfortunately a large percentage of these contain non-native species to Britain, like pines, spruces and firs. These 'softwoods' grow far more quickly than native 'hardwoods' such as oak, and therefore provide a better commercial income for foresters. However, these introduced trees support a far less diverse fauna than do native trees and they are often planted so close together that they shade out many species of plant, especially those that require direct sunlight to grow. Pine needles are also very acidic and slowly acidify the ground, again to the detriment of many species that cannot survive on this type of soil.

Large numbers of native trees have also been planted in the county, not only as woodlands but along road-sides etc.. Although this is good for our wildlife, it will take many hundreds of years before they can support the numbers of species that ancient woodlands do. They can be seen as an investment in our future, and the future of the many species of flora and fauna that cannot survive without this habitat.

Urban Habitats

Post Industrial Sites

Post-industrial sites (also referred to as 'brown field' sites) include railway embankments, road verges, derelict industrial sites, slag heaps and waste land. Surprisingly, they are very rich in species diversity, containing many plants and animals that rely upon disturbed ground for their existence. Such species include 'vernal' or 'pioneer' plants that are the first to colonise disturbed areas, for example ragwort, thistles and docks. Many common species of insect are associated with these plants. Small mammals and birds are attracted by the seeds and fruits of the pioneer species and by the abundant insects and other invertebrates that are found there. Thus Wood Mouse, Field and Bank Voles, Woodpigeon, Collared Dove, Dunnock, Robin, Blackbird, Song and Mistle Thrushes, Great and Blue Tits, Wren, Magpie, Carrion Crow, Starling, House Sparrow, Chaffinch, Greenfinch, Linnet and Goldfinch are also commonly observed in these areas.

Clay Brooke Marsh

In the process of natural succession, such post industrial areas would gradually develop into woodland scrub and eventually into mature woodland. However such sites are frequently regarded as eye-sores or as a wasted land resource, and often disappear under new development. A prime example of a post industrial site in Warwickshire is Clay Brooke Marsh (once known as Herald Way Marsh) in Coventry. This is located on the site of former mine-workings and slag heaps but is currently home to many species of insect and bird, and even has wild orchids growing there.

Parks and Recreational Areas

Parks and other recreational areas are usually found in towns and cities and are a vital 'green-space', where people can get a taste of fresh air and peacefulness in the hubbub of modern day life. Many of these spaces are also vital for the survival of the wildlife species that make their home in our urban areas. Large mammals such as Rabbits, Grey Squirrels, Badgers and Red Foxes can be found even in the heart of our largest cities due in part to these green areas, along with spectacular birds such as woodpeckers, Jays and Sparrowhawks.

Old cemeteries such as this one at London Road in Coventry are quiet oases in the heart of suburban Warwickshire, not only for people but for wildlife too

At first glance many of these parks can often look like green deserts, with vast expanses of regularly mown amenity grassland. Yet most of them contain 'wild' corners that are inaccessible to the gang-mowers, where plants and animals can flourish in relative peace. Cemeteries are often managed less intensively than other public areas and are peaceful havens not only for wildlife but for people too. Many contain species such as Tawny Owls, bats and Spotted Flycatcher's - animals and birds that are more often associated with the countryside than towns. London Road Cemetery in Coventry is a good example and well worth a visit, especially on a warm sunny day in the summer.

Gardens

Gardens are a vast resource for wildlife. All sizes and types of gardens can be useful, from window boxes on tower blocks (where Kestrels have been known to nest), to

23

huge suburban gardens that contain copses of trees and wild-flower meadows. Garden flowers are visited by insects like Bumblebees, Honey Bees, wasps, hoverflies, moths and butterflies. In turn, the insects attract birds like the Wren, Dunnock and Robin into the garden. Even regularly mown lawns attract Blackbirds who feed on earthworms, and Starlings who unearth Leather-jackets (the grubs of Daddy-long-leg flies).

It is also likely that garden ponds have been instrumental in protecting our native amphibians, especially the Common Frog. As wild ponds have gradually disappeared from our countryside, garden ponds have stepped into the breach to help take their place.

Many people put food out for the birds in their gardens. This simple act has maintained the numbers of many birds like Blue and Great Tits, Greenfinches and Chaffinches that would otherwise perish in harsh winters. Other less common birds like Jays, Great Spotted Woodpeckers and Siskins have begun to learn that food supplies can be found in gardens, resulting in more frequent visits to these havens, much to the delight of their providers. If gardens are managed as 'wildlife gardens', they can supply refuges for wildlife even in the heart of our cities and immeasurable pleasure to their owners at the same time.

With a little thought and care a host of butterflies and other wildlife can be attracted to gardens, even in the heart of our cities. Here a beautiful Red Admiral is nectaring on a Buddleia bloom

Location Map of Sites and Walks in Warwickshire

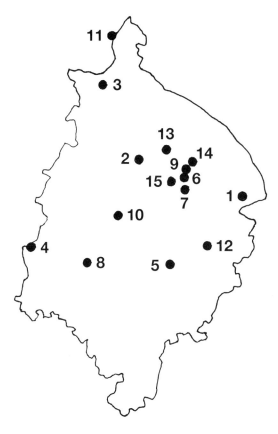

1. Ashlawn Cutting
2. Coundon Wedge
3. Kingsbury Water Park
4. Rough Hill Wood
5. Ufton Fields
6. Brandon Marsh
7. Ryton Wood
8. Snitterfield Bushes

9. Brandon Wood
10. Kenilworth Common
11. Pooley Fields
12. Stockton Cutting
13. Wyken Slough
14. Coombe Abbey
15. Stonebridge Meadows

Site 1. Ashlawn Cutting Local Nature Reserve

Grid Reference: SP516732 (car park). O/S Pathfinder Sheet SP 47/57.

How to get there: Ashlawn Cutting runs south from the centre of Rugby into the Warwickshire countryside. From Coventry, the easiest route to the nature reserve is to go east on the A45 to the village of Dunchurch. Turn left at the traffic lights in Dunchurch onto the A426 and follow this road for approximately one mile. At the roundabout turn right on to the B4429 Ashlawn Road. Follow this past the cross-roads with Church Lane and over the railway bridge. From Rugby go south along Church Lane and turn left at the cross-roads with the B4429.

Public Transport: Buses number 86, 87, 580, 585 and X86 travel to Rugby from Coventry city centre.

Car Parking: There is a small free car park by the allotments immediately after the railway bridge which goes across the cutting.

Admission charges: None.

Disabled access: There is access for wheelchair users from Hillmorton Road and Pytchley Road Bridge via ramps. Other access to the cutting consists of steep steps down the banks.

Opening times: Open all day every day of the year.

Start point: From the allotment car park a path with steps leads down onto the reserve.

Conditions: Conditions are good though it may get muddy under foot in foul weather. Wellington boots may be needed in winter.

Facilities: None on site.

Site guidelines: Please keep to the path along the bottom of the cutting and avoid walking on the grassy banks.

Contact: Recreation and Amenities Division of Rugby Borough Council on 01788 533533 and Warwickshire Wildlife Trust on 01203 302912.

Ashlawn Cutting Nature Reserve is a very pleasant site along a former railway line. It provides a gentle and sheltered walk covering a variety of habitats. The northern boundary of the nature reserve is Hillmorton Road and the southern boundary is Church Lane. The reserve covers a little over one mile of disused railway and around 54 acres of scrub and open grassy banks. The cutting also has an area of marsh and pools near the old Hillmorton Station and these are a haven for breeding newts, frogs and toads. Amphibians live for most of the year on land. They hibernate during the winter in banks, log piles and under the roots of trees but need to return to water in the spring in order to breed. They lay their eggs in the water and these grow into tadpoles which eventually grow legs. In the summer the youngsters move onto land where they become night-time hunters. Amphibians need areas of moist or shady vegetation, such as woodland, hedgerows or grassland, to hunt for the invertebrates that make up their diet.

Disused railway cuttings such as Ashlawn have been rapidly re-colonised by wildlife and now form an important habitat type within Warwickshire, particularly for species that prefer warm, sheltered areas. The cutting is owned by Rugby

During the spring Smooth Newts breed freely in the ponds by the old railway station at Ashlawn Cutting, along with Common Toads and Frogs

Borough Council, who established the site as a nature reserve in 1977. Warwickshire Wildlife Trust manage the reserve for its nature conservation value.

The walk has banks on both sides. These are open in many places and catch the full benefit of the sun. In other places, the scrub consists of a range of native trees. There is a strong population of Rabbits present on the site.

Specialities during the year:
During the spring and summer the banks of the cutting are awash with many bright wild flowers including Cowslip, Green-winged Orchid, Dwarf Thistle, Fairy Flax, Yellow Rattle, Eyebright and lots of Ox-eye Daisy's. Blue Fleabane is a scarce plant in Warwickshire and this can be found on the cutting to the south of the Ashlawn Road bridge. At this time of the year there are also lots of butterflies including Green Hairstreak, Brown Argus and Marbled White. The tadpoles of newts, frogs and toads can be seen in the marshy area and pools near the old station. Birds that visit the site during the summer include Chiffchaff, Willow Warbler, Blackcap and Common Whitethroat.

During autumn and winter the most obvious wildlife to be seen include birds such as Sparrowhawk, Kestrel, Moorhen, Collared Dove, all three species of British woodpecker, Redwing, Fieldfare and Long-tailed Tit.

The Brimstone is just one of many butterflies that can be seen flying on fine sunny days along the cutting during the spring and summer months

28

Site 2. Brandon Wood

Grid Reference: SP399771. O/S Pathfinder Sheets SP 27/37 and SP 47/57.

How to get there: Brandon Wood lies to the south-east of Coventry and south of Binley Woods. From Coventry take the A428 road towards Brandon Village, turn right onto Ferndale Road and follow this road to the junction with Craven Avenue.

Public transport: Buses number 86 and X86 pass along the A428 from Coventry City centre. From here it is only a short walk to the wood.

Car Parking: Park on Ferndale Road or Craven Avenue, but please be aware of residents in the area when parking. Car parking is free.

Admission charges: None.

Disabled access: Access for wheelchair users is via the Ferndale Road gate. Please contact Mr Ray Healey for the key to the gate.

Opening times: Open all day every day of the year.

Start point: The main entrance to the wood is on the junction of Ferndale Road and Craven Avenue.

Conditions: There is a very wide and level loop path (about one third of a mile in length) that is excellent for less able visitors and wheelchair users. A further path of several miles in length is planned for the future. Otherwise the going is firm and mostly dry on the main paths though it can get wet and muddy on the smaller paths.

Facilities: None on site.

Site guidelines: Please keep to the paths and keep dogs under control. Motorbikes and horses are forbidden. Be aware of the danger of causing fires.

Contact: The Midlands District Office of the Forestry Commission can be contacted on 01889 586593. The Chair of the Friends of Brandon Wood, Mr Ray Healey, can be contacted on 01203 543135 and the Vice-Chair, Mr Karl Uhlig, on 01203 544139.

Brandon Wood is a 187 acre site of a former ancient woodland that has been clear-felled and mainly replanted with conifers. It still retains the air of an extremely old woodland however and is very pleasant to walk through, even during the winter, because of its network of wide forest roads. Disabled people will find the going especially easy due to the loop path that has been constructed entirely by volunteers. Important habitats within the wood include clearings, patches of scrub, streams, ditches and many ponds of different sizes. There are several ancient meadows between Brandon Wood and Piles Coppice, and open areas to the west and south.

The wood was once part of an estate owned by Captain Beech of Brandon Hall. It was then sold to the Forestry Commission. Currently, the wood is in the process of being passed onto the *'Friends of Brandon Wood'*, an organisation of local people who have helped to manage the wood for the last decade.

Brandon Wood is a special place to visit because it has a very diverse character with lots of wildlife. It also has a well-deserved reputation for the variety of fungi that grow there. The wood is located very near to Coventry and has easy access for members of the public.

Specialities during the year:

During spring and summer the edges of the open rides contain many varieties of wild flower including Common Spotted Orchid, Meadowsweet, Yellow Flag and Ragged Robin. Woodland

The loop path around Brandon Wood was created especially for the disabled by local volunteers, improving their access to this beautiful wood

butterflies are also widespread and there are good populations of Purple Hairstreak in the tree-tops. You may even glimpse a magnificent White Admiral soaring through the wood on its broad black and white wings. Harmless grass snakes are also often encountered sliding off into the grass by the side of a path or swimming effortlessly across one of the ponds.

During autumn the wood is perhaps best known for its excellent display of fungi. Over three hundred species have been identified including the well-known but elusive Fly Agaric. This bright red toadstool, speckled with white flecks, can be found on sandy soil normally associated with birches. Although a very handsome species, it is poisonous, so don't be tempted to pick it!

Winter can seem very devoid of birds until you come across a feeding flock making their way through the trees. These flocks can be large and often include birds like Long-tailed, Blue, Great, Marsh and Willow Tits. However also look out for Nuthatch, Treecreeper, Chaffinch and Goldcrest. Sometimes these flocks are followed by Great or Lesser Spotted Woodpeckers, so it may be worthwhile waiting until the flock has passed and keeping an eye open for these beautiful black and white birds with their flashes of bright red.

The wood has a well-deserved reputation as a fine place to see a wide range of fungi. A walk through the wood in autumn should turn up many kinds such as this bracket fungus growing on an old tree stump

Site 3. Coundon Wedge

Grid Reference: SP301802 (Staircase Lane). O/S Pathfinder Sheet SP 28/38.

How to get there: Coundon Wedge lies in the north-west of Coventry.

Public transport: Nearby bus routes include the 6, 7, 75 and 900 which pass through Allesley from Coventry city centre. The number 6 and 75 also stop along Kingsbury Road.

Car Parking: On nearby roads in Coventry and Allesley Village, but please be aware of residents needs when parking your car. Car parking is free.

Admission charges: None.

Disabled access: Wheelchair access is very limited.

Opening times: Open all day every day of the year.

Start point: The wedge is accessible from several points including Staircase Lane in Allesley Village, and Dovecote Close and Kingsbury Road in Coundon, Coventry.

Conditions: The footpaths take account of people with special needs such as some elderly and disabled people, for example there are kissing gates instead of stiles. The paths can be wet and muddy in the winter.

Facilities: None on site. A leaflet entitled 'A Guide to Walks in Coundon Wedge' is available free from the Strategic and Local Planning Division of Coventry City Council on 01203 831292.

Site guidelines: Please keep to paths by following signposts and way-markers. This will help you not to stray into areas where you do not have a right of access. Follow the country code.

Contact: Coventry City Council on 01203 833333.

This is a fairly common dragonfly in Warwickshire - the Broad-bodied Chaser. The specimen pictured is a male, distinguishable by its bright blue body. Females lack the blue coloration

Foxglove

Bluebell

The Bee Orchid is one of our most beautiful wild orchids and often turns up in the strangest of places. Its flowers are said to resemble a female bee - hence the name - and they attract amorous male bees hoping to mate. Instead they pollinate the plant!

The Robin is one of our most familiar wild birds and can be found in a variety of habitats from urban gardens to woodland

The Comma is a butterfly that may be encountered throughout Warwickshire. It is typical of habitats like woodlands, tall hedges and mature gardens. Its caterpillars feed on Hop, nettle or elm leaves

The Fly Agaric is the mushroom of fairy tales. Although it is attractive with its white-speckled bright-red cap it can be poisonous - so take care and don't pick it!

Kestrels are a familiar sight, especially along road verges where they hover in search of small mammals. Close-up views like this one reveal the dark eyes surrounded by the brightest of yellow, and show just how beautiful this common bird of prey really is

Coundon Wedge is an area of countryside that penetrates well into the City of Coventry. The wedge has an attractive rolling landscape and is of immense value to local residents as an amenity area, particularly for walking, jogging and horse riding. The landscape is also significant in an historical context, together with the adjoining parishes of Allesley and Keresley, as a fine example of an ancient Arden landscape dating back to at least the Anglo-Saxon period. This farming landscape of small fields surrounded by ancient hedges holds a rich variety of wildlife, in contrast to more modern landscapes of large fields surrounded by wire fences which have little of interest for the nature lover. Coundon Wedge is mainly owned by private landowners and worked as farmland, although Coventry City Council do own some small areas. Please follow the country code when visiting the wedge and keep to the marked footpaths.

The Wedge contains many habitats, including horse-grazed pasture, rough grassland, marshy areas, ponds, hedgerows, scrub, mature trees and small patches of woodland. The River Sherbourne and North Brook both flow through the site and add significantly to its wildlife value. Staircase Lane in the west has some particularly stunning old oak trees along the ancient sunken track-way.

Staircase lane is an ancient sunken lane that has some spectacular old oak trees with exposed roots. This is how many of the lanes in the Arden landscape of Coundon Wedge may once have looked

The most commonly seen mammal on the wedge is the Rabbit. This is often thought of as a native animal, probably because it is such a common sight in the British countryside. In fact the Rabbit was introduced to Britain by the Norman's just after their invasion. They can now be found almost everywhere from the Scilly Islands in the north of Scotland to the Channel Islands in the south and have a major impact on our wild places by grazing the vegetation and keeping it low. Rabbits are a major source of food for other animals such as weasels, stoats and foxes, and are also the main prey of the

Polecat. The Polecat is a large member of the weasel family which was exterminated in Warwickshire over a hundred years ago. Having retreated to refuges in Wales, they are now spreading eastwards back into the lowlands of England, and have made a recent return to the Warwickshire countryside.

Rabbits are common mammals that can be seen almost anywhere in the countryside. The best time to watch them is usually around dawn or dusk although they will come out in the daylight in undisturbed areas

Specialities during the year:
On warm days in the spring look out for early butterflies like the Small Tortoiseshell, Brimstone, Comma and Peacock nectaring on the flowers of willows. These butterflies have hibernated throughout the winter and now have to feed on energy-rich nectar so that they can breed. Common hedgerow birds like the Robin, Wren, Blackbird and Dunnock will also be in full song as they stake out their nesting territories.

In the summer look out for Little Owls perched on fence posts or in trees. Although they usually lay their eggs in spring, summer is the best season to see the birds as their chicks are large and hungry. At this time the adult birds are continuously in pursuit of slugs, snails, beetles and earthworms to feed their young. Summer flowers will also be out on show and so too will other butterflies like the Small Copper and Common Blue.

In the winter the fields will become crowded with huge flocks of Black-headed Gulls. Search these flocks carefully and you may see some of their larger cousins, such as Common, Herring or Lesser Black-backed Gulls. This is also the time of year when Red Foxes can most easily be seen as they frequently hunt during the day time in the winter months.

Sallow blossoms bloom early in the year and provide a vital nectaring source for many insects coming out of hibernation, including this Small Tortoiseshell butterfly

Site 4. Kenilworth Common Local Nature Reserve

Grid Reference: SP297730. O/S Pathfinder Sheet SP 27/37.

How to get there: Kenilworth Common lies in the north-east of Kenilworth. To get there from Coventry take the A429 to Kenilworth Road and turn left onto Common Lane at Crackley Hill.

Public transport: Nearby bus routes include the 12, 112, 114, X14, X16, X17, and X18 from Coventry City centre. These pass along the Coventry Road. From here it is only a short walk to the common.

Car Parking: Parking can be a problem in Kenilworth so please think of others and park your car sensibly.

Admission charges: None.

Disabled access: Access to the common for wheelchair users is very limited and probably impossible in wet weather.

Opening times: Open all day every day of the year.

Start point: The main entrance is along Common Lane and is well sign-posted.

Conditions: Kenilworth Common is very hilly in places. There is an extensive network of footpaths that run through the site, including part of the Centenary Way. Some of the paths can be steep and muddy so access for less abled walkers may be difficult.

Facilities: None on site.

Site guidelines: There is **no** access for cyclists (including mountain bikes), horses or powered vehicles on the common. Cyclists are restricted to the bridleway that passes through the site.

Contact: Warwick District Council Amenities Department on 01926 450000 or Warwickshire Wildlife Trust on 01203 302912.

Kenilworth Common is a large nature reserve covering thirty acres. Although it is surrounded by residential areas, the common still retains the feeling of the countryside and at times it is hard to imagine that the town is so near. The common is predominantly broad-leaved woodland. However, a small area of open heathland habitat remains where some regionally scarce heather grows amongst the Gorse and Bracken. Heathland habitats are very rare in Warwickshire these days and as a consequence a lot of volunteer labour goes in to protecting this habitat wherever it is still found, especially on the common. The common is cut into two parts by a railway line which provides an unbroken link with the nearby countryside, as well as warm sun-drenched banks that are favoured by insects and plants. Another excellent feature of the site is the Finham Brook which runs along the southern edge of the common. This wonderful brook is one of the cleanest watercourses in the county and has good populations of Bullhead, Minnow, Stone Loach and Brown Trout. Kenilworth Common is owned by Warwick District Council who manage the land in partnership with Warwickshire Wildlife Trust. The common was designated as a Local Nature Reserve in 1991.

At first glance a Slow Worm looks very much like a small snake, but it is in fact a legless and completely harmless lizard. Slow Worms are now extremely rare in Warwickshire

The most outstanding feature of the common is that it is the foremost site for reptiles in Warwickshire. These reptiles include Common Lizard and the Slow Worm. Although it looks very much like a small snake, the Slow Worm is in fact a legless lizard and is quite harmless. It can sometimes be seen basking on the sunny slopes within the common but more often than not, all that you will see of them is their tail, as they disappear into the undergrowth. Slow Worms hibernate during the winter in out of the way places under log piles etc.. In the spring and summer they are voracious predators of small invertebrates, especially the small pale-coloured slugs that are hated by gardeners!

The hilly nature of the woodland on Kenilworth Common helps to give visitors the feeling of being deep in the countryside

Specialities during the year:
In spring there is a fine show of wild flowers beneath the woodland canopy. These include Bluebell, Wood Sorrel, Wood Anemone and Lesser Celandine. Look down along the railway cutting and you may see the large yellow butterfly called the Brimstone or the smaller Orange-tip, so-called because the males have bright orange tips to their wings. In the woodland you may be lucky enough to glimpse a sight of the Speckled Wood butterfly as it flits from sunny patch to sunny patch. At this time of year migrant warblers will be returning from spending their winter in Africa and you may hear the lovely songs of Blackcap or Garden Warbler, joined by our resident Blackbirds, Song Thrushes, Robins and Dunnocks.

Summer is the time to keep your eyes open for the famous reptiles of the common. They can be hard to locate, but if you do see one, please do not disturb it or attempt to pick it up. This is the only place in Warwickshire where you can find all of the reptiles recorded in the county, and species like the Slow Worm are extremely rare and so are best left alone. If you are walking by the brook watch out for Moorhens and Mallards with their young. If you are lucky you may see the brilliant blue and orange flash of a Kingfisher as it flies by.

When the trees are bare of leaves in winter, it is a good time to spot the birds of the woodland. These include Sparrowhawk, Tawny Owl, Green and Great Spotted Woodpeckers, Nuthatch, Treecreeper, Jay and Chaffinch.

Site 5. Kingsbury Water Park

Grid Reference: SP203960. O/S Pathfinder Sheet SP 29/39.

How to get there: Kingsbury Water Park is in the north of Warwickshire approximately five miles south of Tamworth and ten miles north-east of Birmingham. From Coventry take the B4098 towards Tamworth. At the southern edge of Kingsbury village turn left at the roundabout onto the A4097, then right at the next roundabout onto Bodymoor Heath Lane. The park is on the right and is well sign-posted.

Public transport: Bus numbers 116, X75 and X79 from Birmingham to Tamworth stop in Kingsbury Village. From here it is only a short walk down by the church and over the river footbridge to the water park. None of these buses run on Sundays.

Car Parking: There are two entrances: The first is where the visitors centre is located (car parking fee of £2.00); the Broomey Croft entrance is further along the lane (car parking fee of £1.50) and this is where the bird hides and nature reserve are located. Car parks can be found throughout the site.

Admission charges: None except car parking fees.

Disabled access: The roads within the park are suitable for wheelchairs. There are disabled toilet facilities and a single *Easi-rider* is available free of charge but must be booked 24 hours in advance. There are also level footpaths that can be used by wheelchair users.

Opening times: These vary during the year: Jan 8-4; Feb 8-5; March 8-6; April 8-6.30; May 8-7.30; June 1st-15th 8-8.30; June 16th-30th 5.30-8.30; July 5.30-8.30; Aug 6.30-7.30; Sept 7-6.30; Oct 8-5.30; Nov 8-4; Dec 8-4.

Start point: A large nature reserve is accessible from the Broomey Croft entrance to the park or by walking under the M42 from the main portion of the park.

Conditions: There is an excellent network of roads and footpaths throughout the park. Less abled walkers will find very little difficulty. Paths in remoter areas may be muddy.

Facilities: There is a visitors centre with toilets, a shop and the Old Barn Coffee Shop (April - Sept open 7 days a week; other times of the year only open at weekends). A wide range of leaflets are available at the park.

Site guidelines: Dogs are welcome but please keep them under reasonable control, especially around the nature reserve, where they need to be on a lead. Bathing and paddling are not permitted.

Contact: Country Parks Information Service on 01827 872660.

Kingsbury Water Park lies in the Tame Valley and is owned and managed by Warwickshire County Council. The park forms part of a chain of wetland habitats which stretch for some twelve miles along the valley and which are of considerable value to wild birds. The park is exceptional for its range of bird life, from passage migrants in the spring and autumn, to breeding birds and over-wintering wildfowl on the lakes. The park was opened in 1975 when it consisted of just a single field and a lake. Since then it has grown enormously and now covers over 630 acres. Nearly all of the park was once worked for gravel and it now consists of a vast complex of around thirty lakes formed from the former gravel pits. Apart from the lakes there are also large areas of grassland, marsh, willow and Alder carr, and deciduous woodland.

The vast areas of open water make the park a relaxing place to spend a few hours and to see some wonderful wildlife

The water park is used extensively for recreational pursuits, including walking, cycling, fishing, sailing and wind-surfing. There is even an adventure playground for the kids. Disabled visitors are especially well catered for throughout the park. For bird-watchers and nature lovers there are three bird-watching hides overlooking Cliff Pool Nature Reserve and these give excellent views of water birds. There is also a nature trail and seasonal walks with interpretative leaflets to accompany them.

44

Specialities during the year:
There have been over 220 bird species recorded at Kingsbury Water Park. In the spring and autumn look out for passage migrants such as Little Ringed and Ringed Plovers, Greenshank, Ruff, Spotted Redshank, Temminck's and Little Stints and Common and Green Sandpipers. Birds of prey also pass through at this time of year and it is sometimes possible to see Osprey, Marsh and Hen Harriers and Buzzard.

During the summer there are many resident breeding birds that are fairly unusual for Warwickshire including Shoveler, Ruddy Duck, Gadwall and Shelduck. There are also a small number of breeding pairs of Mute Swan. Canal Pool is an eighteen acre lake with a small island. A colony of around thirty pairs of Common Terns have bred on the island since 1980. This is the third largest inland colony of this species in Britain.

Winter at the water park is the best time of the year to see some of the wonderful array of water birds that take haven here

Winter sees an influx of water fowl to the lakes including Pochard, Mallard, Wigeon, Teal and Goldeneye, along with up to one hundred Cormorants. Great Crested and Little Grebes, Coot, Moorhen and Canada Geese are also present in high numbers. Up to six Short-eared Owls have been recorded hunting over the marshes.

Site 6. Pooley Fields Nature Trail

Grid Reference: SK250043. O/S Pathfinder Sheet SK 20/30.

How to get there: The nature reserve is in the extreme north of the county just to the east of Tamworth. From Coventry take the M42 and leave at junction 10, taking the A5 towards Tamworth. Turn left onto the B5080 to Stonydelph then right at the roundabout onto the B5000 towards Polesworth. Next turn first left onto Robey's Lane. From Tamworth take the B5000 and just before Polesworth turn left onto Robey's Lane.

Public transport: Several buses travel to Tamworth from Birmingham (about a three mile walk away from the nature reserve.). There are also railway stations in Polesworth and Tamworth.

Car Parking: The Alvecote Priory Country Park car park is along Robey's Lane, on the right hand side of the road before the bridge over the Coventry Canal. Car parking is free.

Admission charges: Free.

Disabled access: None to wheelchairs.

Opening times: Car park opens at 9am. Nature trail open all day every day of the year.

Start point: To get to the start of the Pooley Fields nature trail, go on foot from the car park up Robey's Lane and turn right between the canal and railway bridges.

Conditions: Moderate going for less abled walkers. Can be extremely muddy in wet weather.

Facilities: None on site. Alvecote Pools Nature Reserve Guide (includes Pooley Fields) is available from Warwickshire Wildlife Trust.

Site guidelines: Please keep to the way-marked nature trail so that other areas are left undisturbed. Keep dogs on leads at all times.

Contact: Warwickshire Wildlife Trust on 01203 302912.

Pooley Fields Nature Trail covers 109 acres which are leased from British Coal Opencast by Warwickshire Wildlife Trust. The site was once mined for coal and is now an excellent example of a post industrial habitat. Everywhere you look you can see how the landscape has been influenced by the mining activity, from the large coal slag heaps to the poor quality of the colliery spoil which makes up the soil on site. However nature has taken over resulting in a re-colonisation of the site. There are now extensive reed-beds, fen, marsh, Alder and willow carr, birch scrub, oak woodland, colliery spoil heaps, open water and flooded pasture. The boundaries of the reserve are dominated by three forms of transportation - the railway to the north, Coventry Canal to the south and the M42 to the east.

There is a 'way-marked' nature trail through Pooley Fields which takes you through all of the main habitats on the reserve. The pools, together with those of the adjacent Alvecote Pools Nature Reserve, are possibly the most important site in Warwickshire for the magnificent Mute Swan, with many pairs nesting during the summer. In July and August large numbers of swans arrive to moult in the safety provided by the large expanses of open water. These impressive birds, which are the largest in Britain, are a familiar sight on canals, rivers, lakes and reservoirs. The sight of these birds, so graceful and yet so powerful, evokes a special place in the heart of the public.

The Mute Swan needs no introduction as one of our most stately, largest and popular wild birds

But their lives are not so trouble-free as might be expected and many swans die before they can reach maturity. Large numbers have been killed by oil-spills in the past, but the greatest problem today appears to be over-head wires which kill several birds each year. In spite of the dangers that face them, Mute Swans are doing well and it was estimated in 1991 that there were at least 27,000 swans living wild in Britain.

Specialities during the year:
In spring the site comes alive with bird song from warblers returning from their winter quarters in Africa. Nine species have been recorded in the area, including Chiffchaff, Common Whitethroat, Lesser Whitethroat, Blackcap and Willow, Reed, Garden and Grasshopper Warblers. Newts, frogs and toads are common in the pools and wetland areas.

Summer is a good time to keep an eye open for the chicks of breeding birds on the pools accompanied by their parents. You may well see Little and Great Crested Grebes, Mute Swan, Pochard and Tufted and Ruddy Ducks. The site is also important for its wetland plants, especially Southern Marsh Orchid, Water Crows-foot, Marsh Wound-wort, Yellow Flag, Meadowsweet and the insect-eating Greater Bladderwort. The Ringlet butterfly can be seen flying on the site between late June and August, and is quite uncommon in north Warwickshire.

In winter look out for mammals. There are populations of Weasels and Stoats on the reserve, but you are most likely to see the larger chocolate-brown (it looks black when wet) American Mink swimming around the edge of the pools or darting across the path. There may also be over-wintering waterfowl on the pools.

The Ringlet is an uncommon butterfly in north Warwickshire. It prefers damp, water-logged spots where there are tall patches of wild grasses for its caterpillars to feed on

Site 7. Rough Hill Wood Nature Reserve

Grid Reference: SP053638. O/S Pathfinder Sheet SP 06/16.

How to get there: The wood lies on the county boundary with Worcestershire, just south of Redditch. From Coventry take the A46 past Stratford, then join the A435 towards Studley. Turn left off this road onto the A448 towards Redditch.

Public transport: Bus numbers 146 and 176 run to Redditch from Birmingham. There is also a railway station in Redditch (about three miles to the wood).

Car Parking: There is a lay-by beside the wood. A stile gives access to the wood. There is also a car park in the wood on the right, off the A448 Studley to Redditch road. The car park is padlocked and only members of the Warwickshire Wildlife Trust have normal access to it. Car parking is free.

Admission charges: None.

Disabled access: Wheelchair access is very limited because of the steepness of the slopes within the wood.

Opening times: Open all day every day of the year.

Start point: The path leading from the Warwickshire Wildlife Trust car park.

Conditions: The foot-paths can be steep in places and they do get extremely muddy. Less abled walkers will find the going very difficult.

Facilities: None on site.

Site guidelines: Please keep dogs under control.

Contact: Warwickshire Wildlife Trust on 01203 302912.

Rough Hill Wood Nature Reserve is a Site of Special Scientific Interest. It consists of fifty acres of ancient deciduous woodland adjacent to Wirehill Woods Country Park in Worcestershire. Early records from 1240 indicate that Rough Hill Wood was once a part of the Royal Forest of Feckenham. Warwickshire Wildlife Trust purchased the wood in 1994 and now manage it for the benefit of its wildlife. The character of the wood is unusual for Warwickshire as it is situated on a steep slope and there are large numbers of Sessile Oaks. The latter can be identified by their longer stalk to leaf distance and their shorter acorn stalks. Sessile Oak trees have their stronghold in this north-west part of the county.

The character of the wood changes noticeably as you climb to the top of the ridge on which it lies. Lower down are heavy, damp soils with small pools and marshy areas dominated by Hazel and Ash trees. At the top of the slope the soil is more sandy and you can find Heather and Bilberry, both of which are uncommon in most of Warwickshire's woodlands. A picturesque stream runs through the wood and there are the remains of old sand pits from the 1940s.

Rough Hill Wood is a prime ancient woodland site which is alive with wildlife and a real pleasure to visit

It is thought that the unusual character and different structure of this woodland (with the presence of the Sessile Oaks and Bilberry) has led to some sightings of birds that are far more typical of upland woodlands in the west of Britain. For example both Wood Warbler and Buzzard have been noted at Rough Hill Wood in the past. The Wood Warblers song is a beautiful shivering trill. The spiralling

The Buzzard appears to be making a come-back into Warwickshire with more sightings of this large bird of prey each year. Buzzards will hunt anything from a beetle to a full-grown Rabbit

courtship display flight of the male, in and below the canopy, is hard to forget once it has been seen.

The Buzzard, in contrast, is a large bird of prey. The species was once common throughout Britain but was persecuted heavily by gamekeepers during the early parts of this century. It also suffered badly when myxomatosis virtually wiped out their main prey animal, the Rabbit, in the 1950s. Today there are regular but scattered reports of Buzzards in Warwickshire and at least one pair have bred recently in the county. Buzzards nest on cliffs or in tall trees and hunt for small mammals and Rabbits by circling high in the air or perching on exposed branches or fence posts to scan the ground below.

Specialities during the year:
In spring and summer the woodland floor is bright with the flowers of Bluebell, Wood Anemone, Lesser Celandine and violets. Once the leaves appear on the trees, flowering plants are harder to find but include Sanicle and two orchids that are scarce in Warwickshire - Broad-leaved and Violet Helleborines. Woodland butterflies like the Speckled Wood can be seen spiralling in patches of sunlight, and

you may be lucky and see a Wall Brown butterfly resting on one of the paths.

Autumn is the time for fungi at Rough Hill Wood and many varieties can be seen including the familiar red and white Fly Agaric and the Oyster Mushroom growing in large clumps on the trunks of trees.

As with most woodlands in winter, birds appear to be scarce until you come across a wandering feeding flock that may contain a number of different species like tits, Treecreeper, Nuthatch, Goldcrest and Great Spotted Woodpecker. Watch out for the sudden dart of a hunting Sparrowhawk as it flies effortlessly through the tangled branches of trees, hoping to startle an unwary bird.

Heather is now a rare sight in Warwickshire

Site 8. Stockton Cutting Local Nature Reserve

Grid Reference: SP437651. O/S Pathfinder Sheet SP 46/56.

How to get there: Stockton Cutting is in the east of Warwickshire, north-east of Southam. From Coventry take the A423 to Southam. After passing through Long Itchington and just before you reach Southam, turn left onto the A426 towards Dunchurch and Rugby. The entrance to Stockton Cutting is on the right just before you cross the bridge over the Grand Union Canal.

Public transport: None.

Car Parking: You can park your car on the adjacent verge of the A426, or alternatively there is a small car park below the canal bridge.

Admission charges: None.

Disabled access: There is no access for wheelchair users.

Opening times: Open every day of the year.

Start point: Access to the nature reserve is via a stile on the east side of the road. There are signs but these are rather small and not that obvious.

Conditions: The paths through the nature reserve are quite steep in places (there are steps in the steepest parts) and there are a few stiles to be crossed, so less abled walkers may have difficulty.

Facilities: None on site. Stockton Cutting Nature Reserve Guide is available from Warwickshire Wildlife Trust.

Site guidelines: Please keep to the paths and keep dogs under control.

Contact: Warwickshire Wildlife Trust on 01203 302912.

Stockton Cutting is a small site that covers around fourteen acres. Despite its small size it enjoys a wealth of wildlife out of all proportion to its size. The site is a section of abandoned railway cutting with an adjacent spoil-bank, which lies on limestone and Blue Lias clay. This setting provides rich and varied habitats, including large areas of grassland on the spoil-bank, tall herb, hawthorn scrub, sheltered sunny clearings, mature woodland and a small, flooded quarry with very steep cliff-like banks. Such calcareous substrate is scarce in Warwickshire and very floristically rich. The railway cutting is owned by Warwickshire County Council and has been designated as a Local Nature Reserve. The spoil-bank and abandoned railway line are owned by Rugby Portland Cement Company Limited. All of the nature reserve is a Site of Special Scientific Interest. Warwickshire Wildlife Trust is licensed to manage the cutting and part of the spoil-bank with an access agreement for the remainder.

The area of Warwickshire around Stockton Cutting has a recent history of quarrying for lime although the land was largely used for the grazing of cattle and sheep up until the seventeenth century. In 1800 the Grand Union Canal was opened and by 1834 at least two quarries were worked in the area. Subsequently several quarries were opened and worked until 1944 when Rugby Portland Cement decided to concentrate its efforts at the Southam and Bishop's Itchington works. The railway line was finally closed in 1958.

Marbled White butterfly

The butterflies of Stockton Cutting are one of its finest features. At least thirty one species have been recorded including several that are scarce in the county such as Grizzled and Dingy Skippers, Wood White, Green Hairstreak and Marbled White. The latter species is generally restricted to the south of England and prefers tall unimproved grassland where its caterpillars feed on wild grasses. The adults with their distinctive black and white markings fly from June until early September and can be found in large numbers nectaring on Knapweed and Field Scabious.

Specialities during the year:

Spring and summer are the best times to visit Stockton Cutting. There is a magnificent range of lime-loving plants to be found at these times of year. These include Greater Butterfly Orchid, which can be seen on the bank by the steps leading into the reserve, Common Spotted Orchid, Common Twayblade, Cowslip, Wild Thyme, Yellow-wort, Milkwort, Eyebright, Small Toadflax, Common Centaury, Woolly Thistle, Restharrow, Kidney Vetch and Autumn Gentian. Butterflies, other than those mentioned above, include Brimstone and White-letter Hairstreak. Look out too for day-flying moths like Mother Shipton, Burnet Companion and Six-spot and Narrow-bordered Five-spot Burnets. The White-legged Damselfly is a scarce insect in Warwickshire but has been recorded occasionally.

Winter is less interesting for visitors, but the nature reserve does support a small population of common birds including woodpeckers.

The Common Twayblade, with its small greenish flowers and low-growing leaves, is a wild orchid that is easily over-looked

55

Site 9. Ufton Fields Nature Reserve and Country Park

Grid reference:	SP378615. O/S Pathfinder Sheet SP 26/36.
How to get there:	The nature reserve is located four miles to the south-east of Royal Leamington Spa. From Leamington take the A425 towards Southam. At Ufton village turn right at the roundabout into Ufton Lane and head towards Harbury. The road turns sharply to the left and then sharp right and the car park is just along on the left hand side.
Public transport:	None.
Car Parking:	The car park is locked from Monday to Saturday (Warwickshire Wildlife Trust members have access) but is open to the public on Sundays from 11am to 4pm and Bank Holiday Mondays. Car parking is free.
Admission charges:	None.
Disabled Access:	There is access for wheelchairs but the going is occasionally rough and it may be difficult to negotiate the paths at certain times of the year. Two bird hides have access for wheelchairs.
Opening times:	Open all day every day of the year, but beware of opening times for the car park.
Start Point:	The path leading from the car park.
Conditions:	There is an all-weather footpath so the going is moderate throughout the year. Less abled walkers should not have too much trouble.
Facilities:	None on site. Ufton Fields Nature Reserve Guide is available from Warwickshire Wildlife Trust.
Site guidelines:	Please keep to the paths and keep dogs on a lead as sheep may be grazing.
Contact:	Country Parks information service on 01827 872660 and Warwickshire Wildlife Trust on 01203 302912.

Ufton Fields Nature Reserve was designated as a Site of Special Scientific Interest in 1972. The site lies on limestone deposits and is particularly well-known for its very rich flora, especially orchids, though other wildlife like dragonflies, butterflies and birds are well represented. The nature reserve comprises 77 acres of coniferous and deciduous woodland, scrub, flower-rich grassland, reed-beds and several pools. There is an all-weather path, about one and a third miles long, which takes you through all of the major habitats on the reserve. Ufton Fields was given to Warwickshire County Council in 1970 and they now use the site as a country park. It is managed as a nature reserve under a licence agreement with the Warwickshire Wildlife Trust.

The grassland supports many small mammals such as shrews, mice and voles, and these in turn are preyed upon by the reserves resident population of Tawny Owls. The Tawny Owl is Britain's most common owl and it is found in varied habitats which range from urban parks to ancient woodland. It is the adults of this species that make the classic 'to-whit-to-whoo' call, particularly at dusk and dawn. During any month of the year the owls are mostly active at night but it is possible to see them during the day especially in spring or early summer when they have a hungry brood to feed and they are forced to hunt in the daylight. Roosting birds

An adult Tawny Owl is well-camouflaged and unlikely to be spotted during the day as it roosts motionless in a tree. Sometimes they are 'mobbed' by small noisy birds trying to drive them away, but more often than not the owls ignore them

can be located by listening out for the angry calls of smaller birds who often mob them during the day.

Another animal that is present at Ufton is the harmless Grass Snake. This is Britain's largest terrestrial reptile, occasionally up to two metres in length. The snake has an olive-green body with dark streaks or spots on its flanks and a distinctive yellowish collar behind the head. Grass Snakes lay eggs in piles of rotting vegetation or manure where they are incubated by the heat of decomposition. They eat small mammals, amphibians and even fish, and are very accomplished swimmers. They are sometimes found by the pools or in the damper areas of the reserve.

The Grass Snake is quite harmless and is our commonest snake. It often 'basks' in the sun on a warm day but tends to glide off into the vegetation, when disturbed, before we can see it

Specialities during the year:
In the spring and summer the reserve is best for its lime-loving plants, especially Yellow Wort, Adder's Tongue Fern, Ox-eye Daisy, Wild Basil and six species of Orchid - including Greater Butterfly, Bee, Early Purple, Common Spotted and Twayblade. There is also plenty of wildlife to look for including many dragonflies and butterflies. Warblers are well represented but also listen out for another African migrant, the Turtle Dove. This small, fairly uncommon dove, makes a distinctive and soothing 'turr, turr' call and prefers the open woodland and scrub.

Winter is the best time to see the mammals of Ufton Fields which include Red Fox, Rabbit, Grey Squirrel and Chinese Muntjac. The pools hold resident populations of Little Grebe, Mallard, Moorhen and Coot, while winter visitors may include Tufted Duck, Teal and Pochard. Woodcocks are sometimes seen in the woodland as well as large flocks of Redpoll, Siskin, Redwing and Fieldfare.

Adder's Tongue Fern

Site 10. Wyken Slough Local Nature Reserve

Grid reference: P362835. O/S Pathfinder Sheet SP 28/38.

How to get there: The nature reserve is located on the north-east edge of Coventry off the Alderman's Green Road.

Public Transport: The nearest bus routes are the 31A, 31C, 37, 47 and 51 from the city centre. These buses all stop along Alderman's Green Road. None of these run on a Sunday.

Car Parking: There is a small car park next to Hawkesbury Fields School along Alderman's Green Road. Car parking is free.

Admission charges: None.

Disabled access: Some of the foot-paths are surfaced and are accessible to wheelchair users, allowing close access to the pool.

Opening times: Open all day every day of the year.

Start point: The path leading from the car park.

Conditions: Apart from the surfaced paths the remainder of the foot-paths around the site can be rough and muddy and most are not suitable for wheelchairs. Less abled walkers should have little difficulty in negotiating most of the nature reserve.

Facilities: None on site. Leaflets entitled 'A Guide to Wyken Slough' and 'The Sowe Valley Footpath' are available free of charge from Coventry City Council at the telephone number shown below.

Site guidelines: Follow the country code.

Contact: Strategic and Local Planning Division of Coventry City Council on 01203 831292 and Warwickshire Wildlife Trust on 01203 302912.

Wyken Slough Local Nature Reserve is an integral part of the Sowe Valley Foot-path. This foot-path is a continuous riverside park beginning at Sutton Stop in the north of Coventry, following the Oxford Canal and the River Sowe for eight miles south through the city, and ending at Stonebridge Meadows Local Nature Reserve. The foot-path runs through Wyken Slough just south of the canal. The nature reserve is a lovely quiet place to visit at any time of the year and is well-located in Coventry with very easy access. It covers a large area containing rough pasture and meadows, developing scrub, reed-beds and Wyken Pool, which is the largest expanse of water in Coventry and a haven for waterfowl.

The area around Wyken Slough was mined for coal from the 17th century. After the mines were abandoned in 1863 the area reverted back to farmland and in the late 1860s subsidence from the former mine-workings created the pool and marshy area. In the 1960s the M6 motorway was constructed nearby and the fields between this

The water birds on Wyken Pool. The area around the pool is a tranquil setting for an afternoon stroll

road and the edge of the city became isolated and were abandoned as agricultural land. The area was designated as a Local Nature Reserve in 1991 by Coventry City Council, who own the land. The reed-bed to the north of the pool is managed by the Warwickshire Wildlife Trust.

Wyken Pool has one of the largest swan populations in Coventry and these are joined in the winter by a large concentration of waterfowl. There is also a very impressive gull roost. Most of the gulls are Black-headed Gulls, which in summer have a distinctive chocolate-brown hood, which is reduced to a small black spot behind the eye in winter. In contrast to many of the British gulls, this species is not confined to breeding around the coasts; it also has some fairly large colonies on marshes and other wetlands inland. Such colonies are located mainly in the north of England and in Scotland and most of the gulls that we see in Warwickshire join us just for the winter. Gulls will feed on rubbish tips and will also follow farmers ploughing their fields, returning to their roosts in the evening. Many appear to stay all day at sites like Wyken Pool, perhaps because of the food that is fed to the geese and ducks by visitors.

Specialities during the year:
During the spring and summer there are some fine examples of flowery grassland at Wyken Slough Local Nature Reserve, and you may find Great Burnet and Pepper Saxifrage amongst the grasses. Dragonflies are often abundant around the pool and include some large and spectacular species such as Southern and Brown Hawkers and Broad-bodied Chasers, as well as more dainty damselflies. The butterflies are also abundant especially grassland species like the Meadow Brown, Small Heath and Large and Small Skippers.

The Black-headed Gull is the commonest member of the gull family seen in Warwickshire. In summer their heads are covered with a dark chocolate-brown 'hood', but in winter this shrinks to a small black spot behind the eye, as seen in the photograph

Winter is without doubt the best time to see the many ducks, geese and gulls that visit the nature reserve. There are large numbers of Mallard, Tufted Duck and Canada Goose and these are usually joined by smaller numbers of Shoveler and Pochard.

Walk 1. Brandon Marsh Nature Reserve

Distance: Approximately two miles.

Grid Reference: SP385755. O/S Pathfinder Sheet SP 27/37.

How to get there: Brandon Marsh is located just to the south-east of Coventry. From the Toll Bar End roundabout join the A45 dual carriageway heading towards Northampton. Turn left after 250 yards onto Brandon Lane. The entrance to the reserve is on the right about one mile down the lane. The centre is well sign-posted.

Public transport: Bus number 1 from Coventry City centre terminating at Toll Bar End. The bus does not run on Sundays.

Start/Parking: Brandon Marsh Nature Centre, along Brandon Lane, south-east of Coventry. Free parking. The start point is at the rear of the nature centre.

Admission charges: £1 for non-members of the Trust.

Disabled access: For a disabled walk see the 'National Grid Trail' as advertised in the nature centre. Less abled walkers should not find the going too difficult. Disabled toilets are situated in the nature centre.

Opening times: Open 364 days of the year. 9am-5pm Monday-Friday, 10am-5pm at weekends (opening times may vary when the new nature centre is completed).

Conditions: This is an easy walk along surfaced foot-paths for the most part. It is not suitable for wheelchairs as the paths are narrow in some places. Be aware that the paths can be flooded and impassable at times.

Facilities: The nature centre has displays, toilets and a shop. Leaflets to the reserve are available. New facilities in 1998 include a tea-room which is open during week days.

Site guidelines: No dogs (except guide dogs) are allowed on the reserve to minimise disturbance to the wildlife.

Contact: Warwickshire Wildlife Trust on 01203 302912.

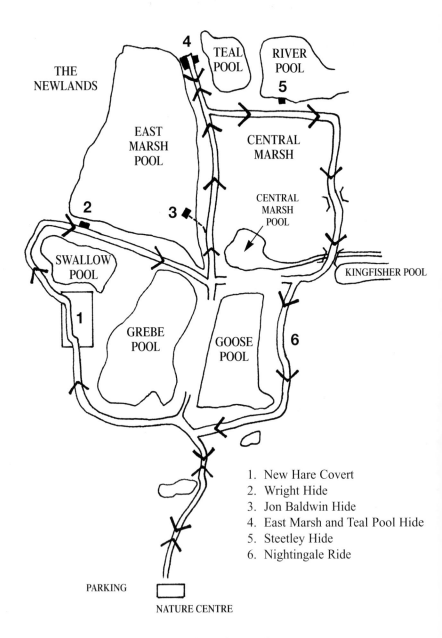

4
TEAL POOL
RIVER POOL
5
THE NEWLANDS
EAST MARSH POOL
CENTRAL MARSH
CENTRAL MARSH POOL
2
3
SWALLOW POOL
KINGFISHER POOL
1
GREBE POOL
GOOSE POOL
6

1. New Hare Covert
2. Wright Hide
3. Jon Baldwin Hide
4. East Marsh and Teal Pool Hide
5. Steetley Hide
6. Nightingale Ride

PARKING
NATURE CENTRE

Map of guided walk around Brandon Marsh Nature Reserve

64

Brandon Marsh was designated as a Site of Special Scientific Interest in 1972. It is an area of approximately two hundred acres which contains very diverse habitats alongside the River Avon. These include lakes, marshes, reed-beds, ponds, woodland, willow and Alder carr, and grassland. The area was agricultural land until the 1950s when underground subsidence from the exhausted Binley Colliery caused a pool to appear on the banks of the Avon. Around the same time sand and gravel extraction from the site was started, and this continued up until 1989. There are now several deep lakes in the disused gravel pits and settling pools. Since 1981 the nature reserve has been managed by the Warwickshire Wildlife Trust.

A view across east marsh pool at Brandon Marsh. This pool is the focal point for many of the water birds that pass through or are resident at Brandon and the hides give splendid views of a variety of species

Route Directions:
From the rear of the nature centre follow the track as it winds down the slope. This is through land that has been planted with a wide variety of native trees and shrubs which will form a new woodland. Just past the small car park take the left fork onto a black cinder foot-path. When this path forks keep to the left and follow this down the steps and over the bridge. Then carry on through New Hare Covert (1).

This woodland was planted around 1800 and has a fine show of Bluebells in the spring. After leaving the wood follow the path around to the Wright Hide (2). As you pass along the path look over to your left and you will see the Newlands, an area of open marshland and willow trees. The Newlands is home to many birds like the Grasshopper Warbler (listen for its high-pitched trilling song in early summer. The birds themselves are hard to see as they sing from within Bramble bushes). In the summer over sixty species of bird breed on the marsh. These include the rare Cetti's Warbler of which there are several pairs. In winter there is also the possibility of a Short-eared Owl hunting over the Newlands or a Long-eared Owl (perhaps several) roosting in the willows around Swallow Pool (on your right). After visiting the hide continue in the same direction. On the right is Grebe Pool. This is a good spot to look out for the Red-Eyed Damselfly which can be found resting on the aquatic vegetation in summer. Look out also for other damselflies and the larger dragonflies all summer long.

Many kinds of dragonflies are seen at Brandon Marsh in the summer months. This is a mating pair of Common Darters, one of our more common species

Turn left at the cross-roads and carry on to the Jon Baldwin Hide, which is located on an island off the track to the left (3). This is an area where you are most likely to see an American Mink as it dashes across the path, or you might be lucky and spot one as it swims in front of the hide. After visiting this hide carry on to the East Marsh Pool Hide (4). All of these hides overlook East Marsh Pool.

This pool was created by sand and gravel extraction and then extended deliberately to increase the amount of open water. At any time of the year you will have impressive views of a range of water birds but winter sees an influx of species onto the pool like Gadwall, Wigeon, Teal, Shoveler, Tufted Duck and Pochard. In hard weather they may be joined by the odd Smew or Goosander. Teal Pool Hide overlooks a shallow pool that was formed by volunteers who hand-built a dam to maintain water levels. During the winter months it lives up to its name and is often filled with Teal and other shallow-feeding ducks. After visiting these hides, return along the same route for a hundred metres then turn left and head for the Steetley Hide over-looking River Pool (5) This is on a small walkway leading off to the left. River Pool is linked with the River Avon and the water levels fluctuate depending on how high the river is. It is worth searching the pool for passage waders, especially Redshank and Greenshank, in spring and autumn.

Continue along the track, crossing two small bridges and passing Kingfisher Pool on your left. At the next fork, turn left along Nightingale Ride (6) and follow this until it emerges from the woodland onto a surfaced track. Turn right on this track and walk past a small pond on your left, then turn left onto the path that leads back up the slope to the nature centre. The sensory garden (behind the nature centre) may be worth a visit on a fine day as this is a good place to look out for common butterflies nectaring on the flowers. Whatever the time of year it is worth keeping an eye open for any of Brandon's impressive list of mammals around the nature reserve. These include Otter, Red Fox, Chinese Muntjac, Weasel and Stoat.

The Red Fox is commonly sighted at Brandon Marsh where they breed most years. Foxes are a much-maligned native predator doing a good job in keeping down the numbers of non-native animals like the Rabbit

67

Walk 2. Coombe Abbey Country Park

Distance: Approximately two and a half miles.

Grid Reference: SP404790. O/S Pathfinder Sheets SP28/38, SP48/58, SP47/57 and SP27/37 or O/S Landranger Sheet 140.

How to get there: Coombe is on the outskirts of Coventry on the B4027 Brinklow Road. Follow the signs from the city centre or from junction 2 of the M6.

Public transport: The number 585 bus from Pool Meadow in Coventry City centre and Clifton Road, Rugby. This bus does not run on Sunday.

Start/Parking: Coombe Country Park, along the A427 Coventry to Brinklow road. Pay and display car park. Orange badge holders have free parking. The start point is at the rear of the visitors centre.

Admission charges: None.

Disabled access: There is one point where the going might be slightly difficult for wheelchairs and help may be needed. The Duck Decoy Trail has a boardwalk with tap rail for the visually impaired. *Easirider* vehicles are available free but must be booked 24 hours in advance. The visitors centre is fully accessible to wheelchairs and has disabled toilets. There is ramped access into the bird hide.

Opening times: 7am to dusk, every day of the year. Visitors centre open 10am-6pm (April to September), 10am-4pm (October to March).

Conditions: This is an easy walk, most of it along surfaced paths.

Facilities: The visitors centre has interactive displays, a bar and restaurant, help desk, refreshments, gift shop and toilet facilities. Leaflets to the park are also available.

Site guidelines: No dogs, except guide dogs allowed in the visitors centre. Dogs must be kept on leads in designated areas of the park; leaflets are available to show where these areas are.

Contact: Coombe Ranger Service on 01203 453720.

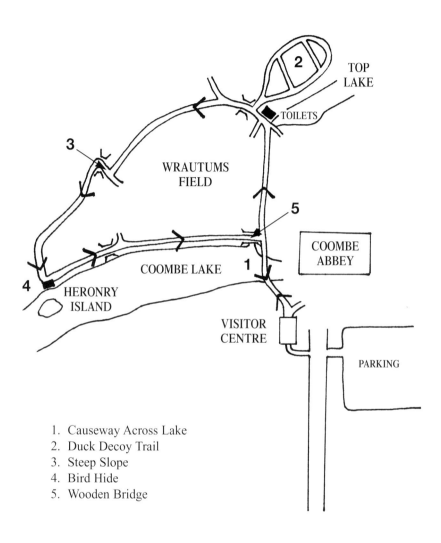

1. Causeway Across Lake
2. Duck Decoy Trail
3. Steep Slope
4. Bird Hide
5. Wooden Bridge

Map of guided walk around Coombe Abbey Country Park

Coombe Abbey was founded by Cistercian monks in 1150. Today the abbey has been turned into a hotel and its four hundred acre grounds, originally designed by Capability Brown, into parkland. Three hundred acres of the parkland grounds are a nature reserve and much of the nature reserve has been designated a Site of Special Scientific Interest. Habitats include lakes, woodland, meadows, heathland, ponds and wetlands.

There is a children's play area and a 'Tarzan trail' for the more adventurous. The park is owned by Coventry City Council.

Route Directions:
From the rear of the visitors centre take the left fork down towards the lake. Cross the lake along the causeway (1). In winter the lake is home to a wide range of water birds which include Great Crested Grebe, Canada Goose, Mallard, Wigeon, Tufted Duck, Pochard, Ruddy Duck, Mute Swan and Cormorant. Coombe is also one of the most important sites in the county for the large-billed Shoveler. Male Shovelers have a striking plumage with a dark green head, white breast and chestnut flanks. The female is much drabber but can still be identified by her heavy shovel-shaped bill. From the causeway you can often get close-up views of some of the more

The Grey Squirrel was originally a native of North America but it is now extremely common throughout Warwickshire and most of Britain. The squirrels at Coombe can be very tame and will let you approach them quite closely - especially if you offer them some food!

common species of water birds. Follow the track and walk on past the wooden bridge on the left, keeping your eyes open for squirrels amongst the trees to the right.

Autumn is the best time to see Grey Squirrels at Coombe as they feed up for the cold months ahead. Some of the squirrels are so used to people that they will take food from the hand if you are patient and keep still. Continue along this track until you reach a junction then turn left past the second lake and the toilets. Just past the toilet block, on the right, is the entrance to the Duck Decoy Trail (2). This is an area

The wooden sculptures of a Sparrowhawk, Woodcock and Badger in Coombe, carved from a single dead tree, set the mood for an enthralling walk in some of the richest wildlife habitats in Warwickshire

that holds a good variety of woodland birds. It is a circular route that will eventually bring you back onto the main path not far from where the trail begins. If you choose to walk around the trail then during the spring listen for the various warblers that have returned from their winter sojourn in Africa, especially the small brown Chiffchaff that has the well-mannered habit of singing its own name from the tree tops - 'Chiff-Chaff Chiff-Chaff'. Other birds, including our resident Wrens, Blackbirds, Robins and thrushes will also be singing to lay claim to their breeding territories. You may also hear the drumming of a woodpecker on a hollow tree or branch. This will probably be the Great Spotted Woodpecker or its smaller cousin

Coombe Country Park has a wide variety of habitats including some delightful woodlands - just right for a stroll on a warm summers evening

the Lesser Spotted. Whether you make a detour around the Duck Decoy or not, follow the main path over the bridge and past the bird sculptures to continue on this walk.

At the fork in the path take the left and follow this path through to an open heathy area. Here you will find red and white Fly Agaric mushrooms growing in profusion during the autumn. When you come to a T-junction (3), go down the slope to the right (this is where it gets a little difficult for wheelchairs - but there is a less steep route if you back-track a little). Go over a small concrete bridge and follow the path around to the left along the edge of the woodland. As you walk through this woodland you will notice that the undergrowth is very thick in places and green, even in the winter. This is because lots of Rhododendron has been introduced in the past and this is very hard to control leading to over-shading of the woodland floor. This woodland is still very good for wildlife though.

Follow this track past a sharp turn to the left and it will lead you to the bird hide (4). This hide has excellent views of the heronry on heron island and has a bird feeding station that is visited by numerous birds including woodpeckers. The park has the largest heronry in Warwickshire with up to fifty pairs breeding and these are easily watched from the hide in early summer. Other breeding birds at Coombe include Sparrowhawk, Tawny and Little Owls and Jay. The Jay is a member of the crow family and is a beautiful pinkish bird with blue and white wing patches and a white rump that is very conspicuous in flight. You will often hear its harsh scolding screech from the depths of the woods.

When leaving the hide turn right and continue until you cross a little wooden bridge, then carry straight on along the edge of the lake. If you stay on this path and follow the lake it will eventually take you over the wooden bridge that you walked past at the beginning (5). Turn right and go back the way you came across the causeway to the visitors centre.

Walk 3. Ryton Wood Nature Reserve

Distance: Approximately two miles.

Grid Reference: SP384726. O/S Pathfinder Sheet SP 27/37.

How to get there: The nature reserve is approximately two and a half miles south of Coventry along the A423 Coventry to Banbury road. The entrance is a small track on the right just before you get to the Bull and Butcher Public House.

Public transport: Bus numbers 570, 580 and X64 run to Ryton-on-Dunsmore from Coventry City centre (about a one and half mile walk to the wood).

Start/Parking: At the end of the track is a small car park. Access is through a padlocked gate that only allows vehicular access to members of the Warwickshire Wildlife Trust. Alternatively, it is possible to park in the car park of Ryton Pools Country Park (see gazetteer) and follow the permissive path through the wood (opening in 1998). Car parking is free in the wood to members but there is a fee at Ryton Pools (£1 at time of writing).

Admission charges: None.

Disabled access: The rides are un-surfaced and not suitable for wheelchairs. Less abled walkers should have little difficulty as there are no steep slopes.

Opening times: Open all day every day of the year.

Conditions: The rides can be very muddy in winter and wellington boots are recommended.

Facilities: None on site. Ryton Pools Country Park has toilets. Ryton Wood Nature Reserve Guide is available from Warwickshire Wildlife Trust.

Site guidelines: Please keep to the paths and keep all dogs on leads.

Contact: Warwickshire Wildlife Trust on 01203 302912.

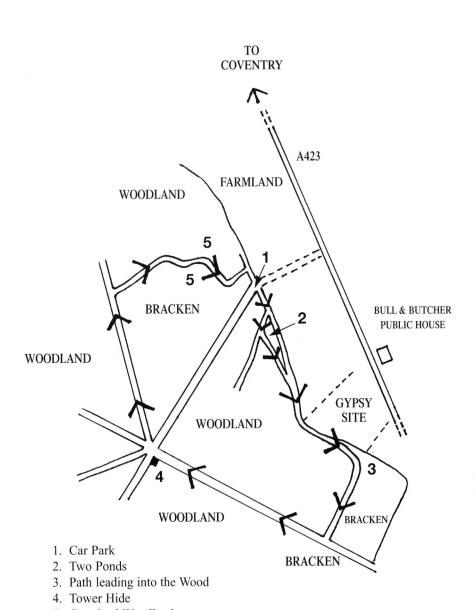

TO
COVENTRY

A423

FARMLAND

WOODLAND

WOODLAND

5

5

1

BRACKEN

BULL & BUTCHER
PUBLIC HOUSE

2

WOODLAND

WOODLAND

GYPSY
SITE

3

WOODLAND

BRACKEN

4

1. Car Park
2. Two Ponds
3. Path leading into the Wood
4. Tower Hide
5. Coppiced Woodland

BRACKEN

Map of guided walk around Ryton Wood Nature Reserve

Ryton Wood Nature Reserve is a Site of Special Scientific Interest. It is a large semi-natural ancient woodland covering 210 acres. The wood is very old indeed. Some of the coppiced Small-leaved Lime trees have been dated at around six hundred years of age. There is also a system of banks and ditches throughout the reserve that may have contained areas of woodland mentioned in the Doomsday Book of the 11th century. The wood was bought by the Warwickshire Wildlife Trust in 1984.

Route Directions:
From the car park (1) follow the track that leads off to the left (when facing down the main ride). This track leads along the edge of the wood and runs through one of the many areas where there is a carpet of Bluebells in the spring.

During spring the floor of Ryton Wood is carpeted with millions of Bluebells and their sweet fragrance fills the air on calm windless days

You may also see drifts of other spring flowers like Primrose, Wood Anemone, Wood Sorrel and Lesser Celandine throughout the wood. Autumn is brightened by the colours of the leaves as they fall to the ground, but also by the huge variety of sometimes brightly-coloured fungi that litter the woodland floor or sprout from tree stumps. Turn right at the next path junction and follow this path for around a hundred yards. Turn left when you see a bridge made out of a split log lying over a ditch. This will lead to two ponds (2). These were created in the 1970s to attract ducks, and Mallard, Tufted Duck, Canada Goose and Moorhen have bred here in the past. This is an excellent site for dragonflies and damselflies in the summer. On the far side of the second and larger pond a path leads back out onto the original track from the car park along the edge of the wood. Continue right along this track until you have passed the gypsy site on the edge of the wood, then turn right onto another track that will lead you into the wood (3). As you follow this track the wood will gradually open out into a large clearing on your left that is high with Bracken in the summer months. In sunny weather, butterflies and dragonflies will sometimes bask on Bracken fronds. When you come to a T-junction turn right and follow this track for several hundred metres. You will notice that much work has taken place to keep the paths open and sunny. This has all been carried out by volunteers who have given their time to maintain the wood. Carry on along this long path until you reach the 'Tower Hide' (4). Here you will find the junction of six tracks, and if you are athletic enough to climb up to the hide it's worth the effort. This is the best place to see 'roding' woodcock flying along the main ride at dusk or dawn during early summer. If you sit quietly and are patient, it is sometimes possible to watch Chinese Muntjac as they come out onto the ride to feed on the bramble along its edge. This tiny deer escaped into the British countryside from Woburn at the beginning of the

Muntjac are tiny deer and they are very secretive. However, you may spot one crossing a ride at any time of the day, although dawn and dusk are the best times. The one pictured is a buck with typically small antlers. Look in any patch of mud at Ryton and you may see the tiny footprints or 'slots' of Muntjac

century and is now the most common deer in the English Midlands. You may be lucky and hear one bark. They sound quite like a dog but the bark is repeated every few seconds. Back home in China they would bark like this to warn other Muntjac of the approach of a Tiger!

The other mammal life of Ryton is rich and is most easily observed during winter when there are no leaves on the trees. You may see Red Fox, Stoat or Weasel, but the most common species that you are likely to come across are Grey Squirrels and Rabbits. The first ride on the right is the main ride and this will take you directly back to the car park. In summer the main ride attracts hundreds of butterflies of which the graceful-flying White Admiral is one of the best. This large butterfly is black and white and can be seen in July, nectaring on Bramble flowers. Other butterflies include two species that have recently been re-introduced to Warwickshire - the Silver-washed Fritillary and the Small Pearl-bordered Fritillary. Both of these have orange-coloured wings. Alternatively take the second right and walk along this track until you see another going off to the right (just past an open clearing dominated by Bracken). Follow this track and it will lead you through the part of the wood that has

Up to six or seven pairs of Tawney Owls nest in Ryton Wood. These are Tawny Owl chicks and in April or May you may be lucky and catch a glimpse of one of these balls of feathers sitting outside a nest hole

been recently coppiced (5). Coppicing is a form of woodland management and is where the under-storey of a wood is periodically cut down to ground level. From the stump or 'stool', a new set of growth spreads out from the outer edge and this is then re-cut on rotation. Growing over this coppice there are often 'standard trees' such as oak which are left to grow tall so they can be used as building timbers. 'Coppice-with-standards' management was generally abandoned earlier this century but has been re-instated in many woods, especially those that are now nature reserves like Ryton. Such coppiced areas are attractive to many species of plants and animals including woodland butterflies such as fritillaries and birds like the Nightingale.

Keep on this track as it turns and winds through the thick coppice until you reach the edge of the wood and another T-junction. From here you can see the car park off to the right.

Walk 4. Stonebridge Meadows Local Nature Reserve.

Distance: Just over three quarters of a mile.

Grid Reference: SP347756. O/S Pathfinder Sheet SP 27/37.

How to get there: The nature reserve is on the southern edge of Coventry. Drive along the east-bound carriageway of the A45 (Stonebridge Highway) towards Tollbar End.

Public transport: Bus number A1 runs from Coventry City centre and stops along Sedgemore Road (about one mile from the reserve).

Start/Parking: There is a lay-by adjacent to the reserve after you pass over the A46 Roundabout. Car parking is free. The start point is from the lay-by.

Admission charges: None.

Disabled access: None for wheelchairs. Less abled visitors may find the going difficult as there are stiles to be crossed.

Opening times: Open all day every day of the year.

Conditions: There are no surfaced paths and the going can be wet due to long grass and muddy. In times of spate the lower part of the path is sometimes flooded.

Facilities: None on site. Leaflets entitled 'A Guide to Stonebridge Meadows' and 'The Sowe Valley Footpath' are available free of charge from the Strategic and Local Planning Division of Coventry City Council on 01203 831292.

Site guidelines: Please keep dogs on leads, keep to the paths through the meadows and follow the country code.

Contact: Strategic and Local Planning Division of Coventry City Council on 01203 831292 and Warwickshire Wildlife Trust on 01203 302912.

Stonebridge Meadows is a large nineteen acre nature reserve that was established in 1987. It contains many different habitats, some of which are extremely uncommon in Warwickshire, such as acidic grassland and flowering meadows. There are also areas of marshy ground, especially by the banks of the River Sowe, which used to form part of the rivers flood-plain. Since the banks of the river have been built up to contain the floods, the marshy areas rarely become inundated with water. Hawthorn scrub is present in many places and provides a valuable habitat for small mammals and nesting birds. A large woodland mainly composed of Alder is also present.

Stonebridge Meadows is owned by Coventry City Council and managed in partnership with the Warwickshire Wildlife Trust.

Route Directions:
The paths are un-surfaced and can be indistinct at times. Therefore we will point out some features to guide you along your way. Cross the stile at the end of the short track leading from the lay-by and turn left, walking through the meadow until you reach the first gate. During spring and summer the meadows at Stonebridge have a wide range of flowering plants amongst the grasses such as Tormentil, Lady's Bedstraw, Meadow Rue, Devils-bit-scabious, Yellow Rattle and Pignut.

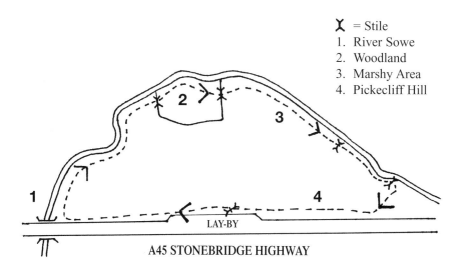

X = Stile
1. River Sowe
2. Woodland
3. Marshy Area
4. Pickecliff Hill

LAY-BY

A45 STONEBRIDGE HIGHWAY

Map of guided walk around Stonebridge Meadows Local Nature Reserve

79

Carry straight on after going through the gate parallel to the line of the A45, until you reach the River Sowe (1). You will notice that as you get nearer to the river the ground becomes progressively wetter (especially in winter). You may see Marsh Marigold and Yellow Flag growing here in the spring and Marsh Speedwell and Meadowsweet in the summer. Keep an eye open for signs of mammals - along this track there are Mole hills, Rabbit droppings and the occasional Fox dropping (grey and twisted with fur in them).

The River Sowe is very rich in wildlife along this stretch. You may see fish like Bullheads or Stone Loaches or even the bright blue flash of a passing Kingfisher - also known as the 'flying jewel'

Turn right at the river and carry on adjacent to it and in the direction of the wood that you can see before you. Cross the stile into the wood (2) and follow the path (it follows the river for a short distance and then turns towards the right). The western end of the wood is mostly Elder and hawthorn scrub with some willows. As you walk on you will notice that the trees get taller - these are Alders - a tree that loves damp ground. This wood was established around 1858 and the Alders were coppiced in four groups on a long rotation, perhaps to provide Alder wood for clogs, which were fashionable at that time. In winter the woodland is best for its birds. You may see a large flock of Siskins feeding in the tops of the Alders. These small birds breed in Scandinavia and visit us during the winter. Often they are joined by Redpolls, a similar sized bird with a red forehead. Other birds that are commonly seen in the reserve include Kingfisher - along the river, Green Woodpecker, Grey Wagtail and Kestrel. Leave the wood by the next stile and again follow the path adjacent to the river.

You will pass a marshy area by the tree-line on your right that is a breeding area for Common Frogs (3). You may see lots of tiny froglets in the summer crossing the path. Cross another stile and walk on. The path gets close to the edge of the river after a while so take care. Along the river look out for water plants like Yellow Water Lily, Water Crowfoot and Common Bulrush. In the summer you may see large damselflies, with a dark blue band across their wings, dancing above the water.

These are Banded Demoiselles and they breed in slow flowing rivers like the Sowe. Cross yet another stile and fifteen metres on at the T-junction in the path, turn

The Banded Demoiselle is one of our most beautiful damselflies. This is a male with the dark blue band across the wings. The female is much duller and lacks the band

right and walk up Pickecliff Hill (4). This is the highest point of the reserve and is acidic grassland. Acid-loving plants such as Harebell and Betony grow amongst the grasses.

Keep a look out here for butterflies like the Peacock, Comma, Small Copper and Wall Brown in the summer months. One notable moth that is common at Stonebridge is the Chimney Sweeper. This is a small black moth that flies during the day in the meadows. It is locally common only in the midlands, being quite rare over the rest of the country. Its caterpillars feed on Pignut. If you visit at dusk or dawn during the summer months you may see Noctule Bats as they feed high over the meadows - listen carefully and you may just hear their high-pitched calls. Follow the path over the hill (parallel to the road again) and through the gate. Carry straight on and you will come to the stile by the lay-by where you started your walk.

The meadows at Stonebridge are alive with butterflies during the summer months. This is one of our commonest butterflies - the Peacock - and these may be seen at Stonebridge from early spring into the late autumn, providing the weather is warm

Walk 5. Snitterfield Bushes Nature Reserve.

Distance: Approximately one and a quarter miles.

Grid Reference: SP200603. O/S Landranger sheet 140.

How to get there: Snitterfield Bushes is located about seven miles south-west of Warwick. From Coventry take the A46 south and leave this road at the sign for the village of Snitterfield. This will take you onto Kings Lane. Follow this lane for a short while then turn right onto White Horse Hill. Follow this road through the village past the Snitterfield Arms towards Bearley. The first block of woodland that you come to three quarters of a mile from the village is the nature reserve.

Public transport: None.

Start/Parking: There is a lay-by on the left and a car park. The car park is padlocked and only open to the members of Warwickshire Wildlife Trust. Parking is free. The start point is across the road from the lay-by and car park.

Admission charges: None.

Disabled access: The northern part of the reserve has an excellent network of concrete paths, most of it left by the RAF after the war. During 1993 this network was extended considerably by the voluntary labour of Trust members and now there is full access for wheelchairs. We recommend that you have help however, as some parts of the paths can be bumpy or muddy.

Opening times: Open all day every day of the year.

Conditions: Conditions are fairly good on the concrete paths but can be muddy on the smaller paths.

Facilities: None on site.

Site guidelines: Please keep dogs on leads at all times (preferably don't take your dog onto the reserve) and keep to the paths.

Contact: Warwickshire Wildlife Trust on 01203 302912.

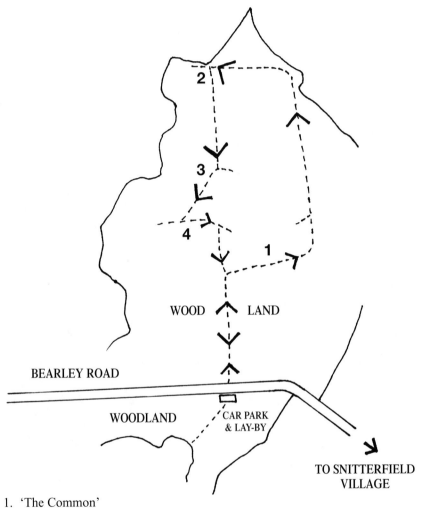

2
3
4
1

WOOD ⋀ LAND

BEARLEY ROAD

WOODLAND

CAR PARK
& LAY-BY

TO SNITTERFIELD
VILLAGE

1. 'The Common'
2. Small Open Area
3. Coppiced Area
4. Recently Coppiced Area

Map of guided walk at Snitterfield Bushes

Snitterfield Bushes Nature Reserve is arguably one of the best woodland nature reserves in the county, yet it has suffered a chequered history of destruction and neglect. The 124 acre site was once part of a much larger woodland that spread to the village of Bearley to the west. In the second world war most of this was felled to build an airfield. The remaining woodland was used to house the RAF's storage sheds and the buildings were linked by a network of concrete paths. This area did not survive long as a woodland and most of the trees were felled during or just after the war.

Snitterfield Bushes Nature Reserve is located on this site and most of the trees that you can see here today have grown since the war. You may find this a hard fact to believe as you walk through the area since it still has the feel of a very old woodland. The abundance of Bluebells, woodland flowers and other wildlife reaffirm this impression. The site is owned by Warwickshire Wildlife Trust.

Primroses flowering early in the year

Route Directions:
From the lay-by cross the road and head up the surfaced path. This path has a profusion of flowering plants growing along the sides in summer, including the unusual Herb Paris (look for its four leaves and white star-like flower on a short stalk). Bluebells and Primroses are present in large numbers in spring, often carpeting the ground beneath the canopy. As you walk along notice the bird and bat

boxes placed on the trees - but please DO NOT DISTURB them. Since much of the wood was felled in the 1940s and 50s there is now a shortage of old trees with holes for birds and bats to roost and breed in, hence the need for these boxes. At the first fork turn right. This will lead you into 'the common' - an open area with a few shallow ponds (1).

In the spring the ponds hold breeding Smooth Newts and the common has a small population of Grizzled Skipper butterflies. Other butterflies that can be seen include

Holly Blue, Common Blue, Brown Argus, Purple Hairstreak, Marbled White and White Admiral. After the common ignore the first path that leads off to the left and continue straight on. In spring and summer keep an eye open for the orchids that are plentiful throughout the wood. There are Greater Butterfly, Early Purple and Common Spotted Orchids, with Twayblade and Broad-leaved Helleborine. Take the next left in a small open area (2).

This open area has a patch of tall herb, mostly willowherbs. After the turn you will notice some Blackthorn scrub along the right-hand side of the path. In autumn this will be heavy with Sloe berries, which are used to make the famous 'sloe gin'. At the next fork turn right. On the right there is a coppiced area that has grown back

Herb Paris is an unusual-looking plant with its four 'cruciform' leaves and star-shaped flowers. They may be found growing in profusion at Snitterfield

very thickly and is now ideal habitat for small mammals and breeding birds (3). At the T-junction turn left. On your right is a much more recently coppiced area (4). You can see the 'stools' of the cut Hazel very clearly. This is the favourite haunt of hunting Kestrels and you may see one hovering in the air as it searches for its prey. Autumn is when the fungi come into their own, and this coppiced area is a good place to look for them. A common species at Snitterfield is the Velvet Shank, a small orangy-brown mushroom that grows in clumps from the bases of trees and cut stumps. This is one of the few mushrooms that can continue growing after being frozen solid during the winter, so it often lingers into the early spring. At the next fork turn right. Keep on the right-hand path at the next junction and this will take you back to the car park. As you walk through the wood you may come across a woodpecker. Snitterfield is a good site to practice your bird identification skills as all three species of British woodpeckers can be found here. The largest of these is the handsome Green Woodpecker - you may glimpse its bright yellow rump as it flies away. They often feed on the ground on their favourite food - ants. Great Spotted's and Lesser Spotted's are harder to distinguish but the Great Spotted is larger than its cousin and has two large white patches on its back. The black back of the Lesser Spotted is barred with white. Walk slowly and quietly around the wood and you may also see the hump-backed form of a small deer crossing the path. This is the Chinese Muntjac.

The wide surfaced paths of Snitterfield Bushes give easy access to most of this lovely woodland, especially to people who are wheelchair bound

Warwickshire's Other Wild Places

Name of Site	Grid Ref.	Ownership	Main Habitats	Main Interest
Baginton Fields	SP358758	Coventry City Council	Grassland, Scrub	Insects, Flowers, Birds
Berkswell Park and Pool	SP244792	Private	Parkland, Pool, Woodland	Birds
Bubbenhall Wood	SP367715	Smith's Concrete	Woodland	Birds, Insects
Burton Dassett Hills Country Park	SP395520	Warwickshire County Council	Hills, Grassland, Woodland	Birds, Mammals
Canley Ford	SP315770	Coventry City Council	Grassland, Woodland, River	Flowers, Birds, Insects
Charlecote Park	SP264564	Private	Grassland, River	Mammals, Birds
Clay Brooke Marsh	SP380771	Coventry City Council	Wetland, Grassland	Flowers, Insects, Birds
Clowes Wood Nature Reserve	SP101743	Warwickshire Wildlife Trust	Woodland	Birds, Insects
Crackley Wood Local Nature Reserve	SP289739	Warwick District Council	Woodland	Birds, Flowers
Deans Green Nature Reserve	SP132682	Warwickshire Wildlife Trust	Grassland	Flowers, Insects
Draycote Meadows Nature Reserve	SP448706	Warwickshire Wildlife Trust	Grassland	Flowers, Insects

Name of Site	Grid Ref.	Ownership	Main Habitats	Main Interest
Draycote Water Country Park and Reservoir	SP468692	Warwickshire County Council	Reservoir, Grassland	Birds
Eathorpe Nature Reserve	SP389687	Severn Trent Water	Wetland, River	Plants, Insects, Birds
Elkin Wood	SP282837	Woodland Trust	Woodland	Flowers, Birds
Goldicote Cutting Nature Reserve	SP247505	Warwickshire Wildlife Trust	Grassland	Flowers, Insects, Reptiles
The Greenway	SP196541 to SP157485	Warwickshire County Council	Grassland, Hedges	Flowers, Birds
Grove Hill Nature Reserve	SP112547	Private	Grassland, Scrub	Flowers, Insects
Hampton Wood Nature Reserve	SP254600	Warwickshire Wildlife Trust	Woodland	Flowers, Insects, Birds
Harbury Spoilbank Nature Reserve	SP384598	Warwickshire Wildlife Trust	Grassland, Scrub	Flowers, Insects
Hartshill Hayes Country Park	SP322945	Warwickshire County Council	Woodland	Flowers, Birds
Harvest Hill Nature Reserve	SP279823	Warwickshire Wildlife Trust	Grassland	Flowers
Hearsall Common and Woodland	SP311785	Coventry City Council	Grassland, Woodland	Birds

Name of Site	Grid Ref.	Ownership	Main Habitats	Main Interest
Henley Sidings	SP147667	Warwickshire Wildlife Trust	Grassland, Scrub	Flowers, Insects
Knowle Hill Local Nature Reserve	SP132682	Warwick District Council	Grassland, Scrub, Woodland	Insects, Flowers
LakeView Park	SP315794	Coventry City Council	Grassland, Scrub, River	Birds, Mammals, Insects
Limbrick Wood	SP289785	Coventry City Council	Woodland	Birds
London Road Cemetery and Whitley Common	SP344778	Coventry City Council	Grassland, Woodland	Trees, Birds
Longford Park	SP353835	Coventry City Council	Wetland, River valley	Birds
Newbold Quarry Park Local Nature Reserve	SP495770	Rugby Borough Council	Pool, Scrub, Woodland	Birds, Insects, Flowers
Old Nun Wood Nature reserve	SP38270	Warwickshire Wildlife Trust	Woodland	Birds, Insects
Park Wood	SP284772	Coventry City Council	Woodland	Birds
Piles Coppice	SP385770	Woodland Trust	Woodland	Flowers, Insects, Birds
Plants Hill Wood	SP280782	Coventry City Council	Woodland	Birds

Name of Site	Grid Ref.	Ownership	Main Habitats	Main Interest
River Arrow Local Nature Reserve	SP086583	Stratford-on-Avon District Council	Grassland, River valley	Flowers, Birds
Ryton Pools Country Park	SP371726	Warwickshire County Council	Pools, Grassland	Birds, Insects
Siskin Drive Bird Sanctuary	SP367748	Coventry City Council	Grassland, Woodland, River valley	Birds, Flowers
Sowe Valley Foot-path	SP362846 to SP346756	Coventry City Council	River valley	Birds, Flowers, Insects
Stivichall Common	SP323775	Coventry City Council	Woodland	Birds
Stoke Floods Nature Reserve	SP375786	Coventry City Council	Pool, Wetland, River valley	Birds, Insects
Stonebridge Meadows Local Nature Reserve	SP347756	Coventry City Council	Grassland, Woodland, River valley	Flowers, Insects, Birds
Ten Shilling Wood	SP291773	Coventry City Council	Woodland	Birds
Tile Hill Wood Nature Reserve	SP280790	Coventry City Council	Woodland	Birds
Tocil Lakes	SP301755	University of Warwick	Pools, Wetland	Birds, Insects
Tocil Wood and Meadow	SP304754	Coventry City Council	Woodland, Grassland	Flowers, Insects, Birds, Mammals

Name of Site	Grid Ref.	Ownership	Main Habitats	Main Interest
Wainbody Wood	SP312751	Coventry City Council	Woodland	Birds, Flowers
Wappenbury Wood Nature Reserve	SP381711	Warwickshire Wildlife Trust	Woodland	Birds, Mammals, Insects, Flowers
Welches Meadow Local Nature Reserve	SP325657	Warwick District Council	Grassland, River Valley, Woodland	Flowers, Birds, Insects
Whitacre Heath Nature Reserve	SP209931	Warwickshire Wildlife Trust	Pools, Wetland, Woodland	Birds, Insects, Flowers
Willenhall Wood	SP371764	Coventry City Council	Woodland	Birds, Insects
Wyken Croft Ecological Park	SP368809	Coventry City Council	Grassland, River valley	Birds, Flowers, Insects

Dawn on Hearsall Common, Coventry

Useful Addresses and Telephone Numbers

Centro Hotline for bus and rail services in Coventry is 01203 559559, and in Birmingham is 0121 200 2700.

Bat Conservation Trust - 15 Cloisters House, 8 Battersea Park Road, London SW8 4BG.

British Butterfly Conservation Society - Dedicated to saving wild butterflies and moths and their habitats. P.O. Box 222. Dedham, Colchester, Essex CO7 6EY. Tel: 01206 322342.

British Herpetological Society - Dedicated to the conservation of Britain's amphibians and reptiles. The Zoological Society of London, Regent's Park, London NW1 4RY.

Herbert Art Gallery and Museum, Jordon Well, Coventry. Tel: 01203 832381.

Plantlife - The Wild Plant Conservation Society. The Natural History Museum, Cromwell Road, London SW7 5BD. Tel: 0171 938 9111.

Royal Society for the Protection of Birds (RSPB) - The Lodge, Sandy, Beds SG19 2DL. Tel: 01767 680551.

Biological Recording Centre for Warwickshire. Warwick Museum - The Market Hall, Market Place, Warwick. Tel: 01926 412501.

Woodland Trust - Britain's largest woodland conservation charity. Autumn Park, Grantham, Lincolnshire NG31 6LL. Tel: 01476 581111.

Further Reading

Nature Reserves Handbook - A Guide to the Reserves of Warwickshire Wildlife Trust. Published by WWT. Brandon, Coventry.

The Nature of Warwickshire - The Wildlife and Natural History of Warwickshire, Coventry and Solihull. Published by Barracuda Books. Birmingham.

Further Information

Warwickshire Wildlife Trust

Warwickshire Wildlife Trust aims to conserve wildlife and natural habitats throughout the county of Warwickshire, including Coventry and Solihull, and to encourage a greater awareness, appreciation and participation in all aspects of nature conservation and the environment.

The Trust works to safeguard local wildlife by
* caring for over fifty nature reserves
    - woods, meadows and wetlands covering over 2,000 acres.
* campaigning for wildlife and the environment
    - helping to protect threatened places and rare species.
* encouraging people to enjoy nature
    - with walks, talks and events in town and country.
* working with schools and community groups
    - promoting a wildlife message to both children and adults.
* promoting ways for volunteers to help
    - with practical conservation projects and local activities.

The mainstay of the trust's growth and development is in its membership, currently totalling over 5,700 members. If you would like to help by joining the Trust as a member, by leaving a legacy, by volunteering your time, or wish to find out more about their work, contact them at Brandon Marsh Nature Centre, Brandon Lane, Coventry CV3 3GW, or telephone the Trust office on 01203 302912.

Acknowledgements

The authors have been assisted in compiling this book by a wide range of individuals to whom we are most grateful. These include Phil Clarke, Steve Falk, Ray Healey, Jim Murray, Richard Oldershaw, Joanna Sutton, Dr Andy Tasker, Joe Taylor, Chris Thomas, Karl Uhlig, Mark Wilkinson and the staff of the New Forest Owl Sanctuary.

We are very grateful for the kind contributions by our very good friends and colleagues Professor David Bellamy and Mr Mont Hirons, and for the photographs of the authors which were taken by Marquita Maynard.

About The Authors

Dr Linda Barnett was born and raised in Cambridge but moved to Warwickshire in 1985 after achieving a PhD in genetics. She now teaches analytical biology and molecular ecology to post graduate students at the University of Warwick. In 1995 she spent a year as a full-time officer with Butterfly Conservation where she co-authored the national species action plans for the eight most endangered butterflies in Great Britain. Linda has had a lifelong interest in photography and wildlife and has married these two interests together to produce the photographs for this book.

Craig Emms has had an interest in wildlife since childhood and has spent the last twenty five years exploring Warwickshire's wild places. In 1994 he achieved a qualification in countryside management and went on to gain a Masters of Science Degree in Ecosystems Analysis and Governance. He is now a freelance ecologist and writer.

Linda and Craig have travelled extensively around the world and have worked on many species of wildlife together. These have included butterflies in Norway and France, and insects, birds and marine turtles on isolated islands in the Indian Ocean. Their research on wildlife in the UK has included moths, butterflies, Tawny Owls, bats, Polecats and Dormice. They have produced many scientific papers covering various aspects of wildlife and achieved a personal goal of discovering a new species to science in 1996. They have been guest contributors for BBC Television and have appeared live several times on BBC Radio West Midlands.

Follow the Country Code

Following the country code will ensure that others can enjoy the countryside as well.

1. Enjoy the countryside and respect its life and work.

2. Guard against all risk of fire.

3. Fasten all gates.

4. Keep all dogs under close control so that they do not disturb cattle, sheep or the wildlife.

5. Keep to public rights of way.

6. Use gates and stiles to cross fences, hedges and walls.

7. Leave livestock, crops and machinery alone.

8. Take your litter home with you.

9. Help to keep all water clean.

10. Protect wildlife, plants and trees. Do not pick wild flowers, leave them for others to enjoy.

11. Take special care on country roads.